Greg Byrd, Lynn Byrd and Chris Pearce

Cambridge Checkpoint
Mathematics
Practice Book
7

CAMBRIDGE
UNIVERSITY PRESS

University Printing House, Cambridge CB2 8BS, United Kingdom

Cambridge University Press is part of the University of Cambridge.

It furthers the University's mission by disseminating knowledge in the pursuit of education, learning and research at the highest international levels of excellence.

www.cambridge.org
Information on this title: www.cambridge.org/9781107695405

© Cambridge University Press 2012

This publication is in copyright. Subject to statutory exception and to the provisions of relevant collective licensing agreements, no reproduction of any part may take place without the written permission of Cambridge University Press.

First published 2012
4th printing 2013

Printed in the United Kingdom by Latimer Trend

A catalogue record for this publication is available from the British Library

ISBN 978-1-107-69540-5 Paperback

Cover image © Cosmo Condina concepts / Alamy

Cambridge University Press has no responsibility for the persistence or accuracy of URLs for external or third-party internet websites referred to in this publication, and does not guarantee that any content on such websites is, or will remain, accurate or appropriate.

The publisher would like to thank Ángel Cubero of the International School Santo Tomás de Aquino, Madrid, for reviewing the language level.

Contents

Introduction 5

1 Integers 7
1.1 Using negative numbers 7
1.2 Adding and subtracting negative numbers 8
1.3 Multiples 9
1.4 Factors and tests for divisibility 10
1.5 Prime numbers 10
1.6 Squares and square roots 11

2 Sequences, expressions and formulae 12
2.1 Generating sequences (1) 12
2.2 Generating sequences (2) 13
2.3 Representing simple functions 15
2.4 Constructing expressions 16
2.5 Deriving and using formulae 17

3 Place value, ordering and rounding 19
3.1 Understanding decimals 19
3.2 Multiplying and dividing by 10, 100 and 1000 19
3.3 Ordering decimals 20
3.4 Rounding 21
3.5 Adding and subtracting decimals 22
3.6 Multiplying decimals 23
3.7 Dividing decimals 23
3.8 Estimating and approximating 24

4 Length, mass and capacity 25
4.1 Knowing metric units 25
4.2 Choosing suitable units 26
4.3 Reading scales 27

5 Angles 28
5.1 Labelling and estimating angles 28
5.2 Drawing and measuring angles 30
5.3 Calculating angles 31
5.4 Solving angle problems 33

6 Planning and collecting data 35
6.1 Planning to collect data 35
6.2 Collecting data 36
6.3 Using frequency tables 37

7 Fractions 39
7.1 Simplifying fractions 39
7.2 Recognising equivalent fractions, decimals and percentages 40
7.3 Comparing fractions 41
7.4 Improper fractions and mixed numbers 42
7.5 Adding and subtracting fractions 43
7.6 Finding fractions of a quantity 44
7.7 Finding remainders 45

8 Symmetry 46
8.1 Recognising and describing 2D shapes and solids 46
8.2 Recognising line symmetry 47
8.3 Recognising rotational symmetry 48
8.4 Symmetry properties of triangles, special quadrilaterals and polygons 49

9 Expressions and equations 50
9.1 Collecting like terms 50
9.2 Expanding brackets 51
9.3 Constructing and solving equations 52

10 Averages 53
10.1 Average and range 53
10.2 The mean 54
10.3 Comparing distributions 55

11 Percentages 57
11.1 Simple percentages 57
11.2 Calculating percentages 58
11.3 Comparing quantities 59

12 Constructions 60
12.1 Measuring and drawing lines 60
12.2 Drawing perpendicular and parallel lines 60
12.3 Constructing triangles 61
12.4 Constructing squares, rectangles and polygons 63

13 Graphs 64
13.1 Plotting coordinates 64
13.2 Lines parallel to the axes 66
13.3 Other straight lines 67

14 Ratio and proportion 68
14.1 Simplifying ratios 68
14.2 Sharing in a ratio 69
14.3 Using direct proportion 70

15 Time 71
15.1 The 12-hour and 24-hour clock 71
15.2 Timetables 72
15.3 Real-life graphs 74

16 Probability 76
16.1 The probability scale 76
16.2 Equally likely outcomes 77
16.3 Mutually exclusive outcomes 78
16.4 Estimating probabilities 79

17	**Position and movement**	**81**
17.1	Reflecting shapes	81
17.2	Rotating shapes	83
17.3	Translating shapes	85
18	**Area, perimeter and volume**	**87**
18.1	Converting between units for area	87
18.2	Calculating the area and perimeter of rectangles	87
18.3	Calculating the area and perimeter of compound shapes	88
18.4	Calculating the volume of cuboids	89
18.5	Calculating the surface area of cubes and cuboids	91
19	**Interpreting and discussing results**	**92**
19.1	Interpreting and drawing pictograms, bar charts, bar-line graphs and frequency diagrams	92
19.2	Interpreting and drawing pie charts	94
19.3	Drawing conclusions	95

Introduction

Welcome to Cambridge Checkpoint Mathematics Practice Book 7

The *Cambridge Checkpoint Mathematics* course covers the Cambridge Secondary 1 Mathematics framework.

The course is divided into three stages: 7, 8 and 9. This Practice Book can be used with Coursebook 7. It is intended to give you extra practice in all the topics covered in the Coursebook.

Like the Coursebook, the Practice Book is divided into 19 units. In each unit you will find an exercise for every topic. These exercises contain similar questions to the corresponding exercises in the Coursebook.

This Practice Book gives you a chance to try further questions on your own. This will improve your understanding of the subject. It will also help you to feel confident about working on your own when there is no teacher available to help you.

There are no explanations or worked examples in this book. If you are not sure what to do or need to remind yourself about something, look back at the explanations and worked examples in the Coursebook.

1 Integers

Exercise 1.1 Using negative numbers

1. Hassan is comparing the temperatures in five cities, on the same day.
   He recorded them in degrees Celsius (°C).
   Write the temperatures in order, starting with the highest.

   −5   5   −4   3   −1

2. Anders recorded the temperature in his greenhouse, in degrees Celsius, at five different times on the same day.

Time	09 00	11 00	13 00	16 00	19 00
Temperature (°C)	−8	−5	2	1	−3

   a What time was the lowest temperature?
   b What time was the highest temperature?
   c What was the difference in temperature between 11 00 and 16 00?

3. What temperature is halfway between each pair?
   a 6 °C and −2 °C   b −12 °C and −4 °C

4. At 08 00, the temperature in Harsha's garden was −5 °C.
   During the day the temperature rose by 8 degrees and then, by 22 00, it fell by 3 degrees.
   What was the final temperature?

5. Sasha writes the height of a point that is 50 metres below sea level as −50 metres.
   a How does she write a height that is 200 metres lower than that?
   b How does she write a height that is 200 metres higher than that?

6. Albert notices that his freezer is getting colder by 4 degrees every minute.
   The temperature now is 6 °C.
   What will the temperature be in 5 minutes?

7. Work these out.
   a −2 + 6   b −10 + 3   c −5 + 5
   d −3 + 13   e −6 + 5 + 3

8. Find the solutions.
   a 2 − 6   b 5 − 12   c −6 − 3
   d −9 − 2   e −3 − 6 − 6

9. Complete these calculations.
   a −3 + 2 − 4 = ☐   b 3 − 5 + 6 = ☐
   c 8 + 3 − 12 = ☐   d −7 + 5 − 3 + 2 = ☐

1 Integers

Exercise 1.2 Adding and subtracting negative numbers

1. Work out the following additions.
   a 4 + 7
   b 4 + −7
   c −4 + 7
   d −4 + −7

2. Work out these subtractions.
   a 8 − 12
   b 3 − −4
   c −5 − −7
   d −6 − −3

3. Find the solutions.
   a 3 − 10
   b 5 + −6
   c 8 + −5
   d −4 − −5

4. Find the missing numbers.
   a 4 − □ = −3
   b −2 + □ = 5
   c □ + −5 = 2
   d □ − 5 = −3

5. The difference between two temperatures is 8 degrees.
   One temperature is 3 °C.
   What is the other temperature?

   There are two possible answers. Try to find both of them.

6. Xavier is thinking of two numbers.

   "The sum of my two numbers is 4. One of my numbers is −6."

   What is Xavier's other number?

7. Copy and complete this addition table.

+	4	1	−2
3			1
−1			
−3		−2	

   The two entries show that 3 + −2 = 1 and −3 + 1 = −2. You must fill in the rest.

1 Integers

Exercise 1.3 Multiples

1. Write down the first five multiples of each number.
   a 9   b 12   c 20

2. a Find the fourth multiple of 6.
   b Find the sixth multiple of 4.

3. From the numbers in the box, find a multiple of:
   a 8   b 10   c 11   d 13.

20	26	32	38	44

4. Find a number between 40 and 50 that is:
   a a multiple of 7   b a multiple of 12   c a multiple of 14.

5. The 16th multiple of 7 is 112.
   a What is the 17th multiple of 7?   b What is the 15th multiple of 7?

6. Find the lowest common multiple of the numbers in each pair.
   a 3 and 5   b 6 and 8   c 10 and 15   d 4 and 7

7. Maha has a number of apples.

   I could share my apples equally among 3, 4 or 5 people.

   What is the smallest number of apples Maha could have?

8. a What is the third multiple of 167?
   b What are the sixth and ninth multiples of 167?

Exercise 1.4 Factors and tests for divisibility

1. Two of the factors of 24 are 1 and 24.
   Find all the other factors.

2. Find all the factors of each of these numbers.
   a 8   **b** 12   **c** 21   **d** 17   **e** 40

3. | 3 6 16 26 36 46 |

   Which numbers in the box have 3 as a factor?

4. There are two numbers between 30 and 40 that have just two factors. What are they?

5. Find the four factors of 91.

6. Find the common factors of each pair of numbers.
   a 12 and 15   **b** 20 and 30   **c** 8 and 24   **d** 15 and 32

7. Find a number that has exactly:
   a 3 factors   **b** 5 factors.

8. | 2571 5427 6622 8568 |

   Which numbers in the box are multiples of:
   a 3   **b** 9?

9. | 2884 2885 2886 2887 2888 |

   From the list of numbers in the box, find the multiples of:
   a 4   **b** 5   **c** 6   **d** 8   **e** 10.

10. What is the smallest number that has 2, 3, 4, 5 and 6 as factors?

11. Find the number less than 100 that has the largest number of factors.

Exercise 1.5 Prime numbers

1. How many prime numbers are less than 20?

2. What is the 15th prime number, if they are listed in order?

3. List all the prime numbers between 80 and 90.

4. Explain why a prime number cannot be a square number.

5. Are these statements true or false?
   a All primes are odd numbers.
   b It is impossible to find three consecutive odd numbers that are all primes.
   c There is only one prime number between 90 and 100.

6. **a** Write 25 as the sum of three different prime numbers.
   b How many ways are there to do this?

1 Integers

7 Find the prime factors of each number.
  a 12   **b** 27   **c** 28   **d** 30

> Prime factors are factors that are prime numbers.

8 Write each of these numbers as a product of primes.
  a 21   **b** 22   **c** 35   **d** 51   **e** 65

9 Why can two prime numbers only have one common factor?

Exercise 1.6 Squares and square roots

1 Find the value of each number.
  a 5^2 **b** 9^2 **c** 11^2 **d** 18^2

2 There is one square number between 200 and 250.
   What is it?

3 Find two square numbers that add up to each of these numbers.
  a 80   **b** 90   **c** 100

4 Look at the pattern in the box.
  a Check that it is correct.
  b Write down the next two lines in the pattern.
  c Use the pattern to work out $51^2 - 49^2$.

$$4^2 - 2^2 = 2 \times 6$$
$$5^2 - 3^2 = 2 \times 8$$
$$6^2 - 4^2 = 2 \times 10$$

5 The difference between two square numbers is 19.
   What are the two square numbers?

6 The sum of two square numbers is 15^2.
   What are the square numbers?

7 There are nine square numbers less than 100.
   Which one has the largest number of factors?

8 Find the value of each number.

  a $\sqrt{9}$ **b** $\sqrt{36}$ **c** $\sqrt{169}$ **d** $\sqrt{400}$ **e** $\sqrt{256}$

9 Is $\sqrt{9+16}$ the same as $\sqrt{9} + \sqrt{16}$?
   Give a reason for your answer.

10 The square root of Eve's age is two more than the square root of Jamil's age.
   If Jamil is 9 years old, how old is Eve?

1 Integers

2 Sequences, expressions and formulae

◆ Exercise 2.1 Generating sequences (1)

1. For each of these infinite sequences, write down:
   i the term-to-term rule
   ii the next two terms
   iii the tenth term.
   a 12, 14, 16, 18, …   b 5, 8, 11, 14, …   c 46, 42, 38, 34, …

2. Write down the first three terms of each of these sequences.

	First term	Term-to-term rule
a	4	Add 3.
b	30	Subtract 5.
c	15	Add 3 and then subtract 4.
d	10	Multiply by 2 and then add 1.
e	2	Divide by 2 and then add 10.
f	12	Multiply by 2, then divide by 4 and then multiply by 2.

3. Copy these finite sequences.
   Fill in the missing terms that go in the boxes.
   a 6, 9, ☐, 15, ☐, 21, 24   b 3, 10, 17, ☐, ☐, 38, ☐
   c 45, ☐, ☐, 27, 21, ☐, 9   d ☐, ☐, 17, 14, ☐, ☐, ☐

4. Write down whether each of these sequences is finite or infinite.
   a 5, 10, 15, 20   b 3, 5, 7, 9, …   c 585, 575, 565, 555

 5. Anders and Tanesha are looking at this number sequence.
   3, 6, 17, 42, 87, 158, …, …
   Is either of them correct?
   Explain your answer.

I think the term-to-term rule is: 'Add 3.'

I think the term-to-term rule is: 'Multiply by 2.'

 6. The second term of a sequence is 10.
   The term-to-term rule is: 'Multiply by 4 then subtract 2.'
   What is the first term of the sequence?

 7. The fourth term of a sequence is 18.
   The term-to-term rule is: 'Subtract 3 then multiply by 3.'
   What is the first term of the sequence?

12 2 Sequences, expressions and formulae

Exercise 2.2 Generating sequences (2)

1 This pattern is made from dots.

Pattern 1  Pattern 2 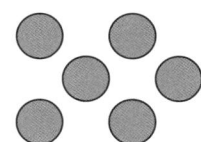 Pattern 3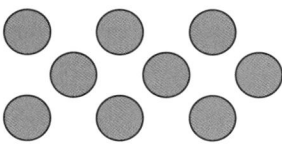

   a Draw the next two patterns in the sequence.
   b Write down the number sequence of the dots.
   c Write down the term-to-term rule.
   d Explain how the sequence is formed.

2 This pattern is made from squares.

Pattern 1 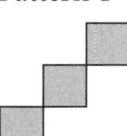 Pattern 2 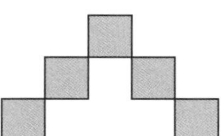 Pattern 3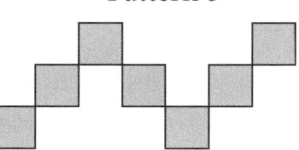

   a Draw the next two patterns in the sequence.
   b Copy and complete the table to show the number of squares in each pattern.

Pattern number	1	2	3	4	5
Number of squares	3	5			

   c Write down the term-to-term rule.
   d How many squares will there be in:
      i Pattern 8   ii Pattern 15?

3 This pattern is made from blocks.

Pattern 1 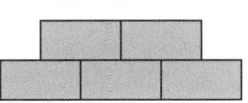 Pattern 2 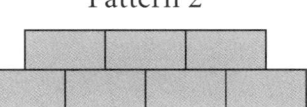 Pattern 3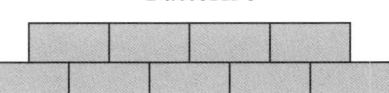

   a Draw the next two patterns in the sequence.
   b Copy and complete the table to show the number of blocks in each pattern.

Pattern number	1	2	3	4	5
Number of blocks					

   c Write down the term-to-term rule.
   d How many blocks will there be in:
      i Pattern 10   ii Pattern 20?

2 Sequences, expressions and formulae

4 Sesane is using dots to draw a sequence of patterns.
She has spilt coffee over the first and third patterns in her sequence!

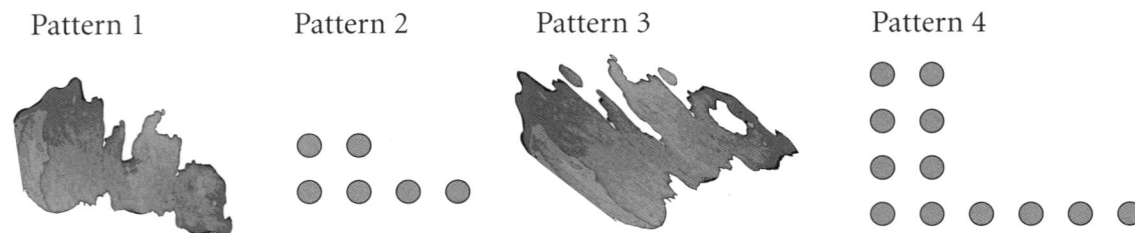

a Draw the first and the third patterns of Sesane's sequence.
b How many dots will there be in Pattern 6?

 5 Alicia and Oditi are looking at this sequence of patterns made from squares.

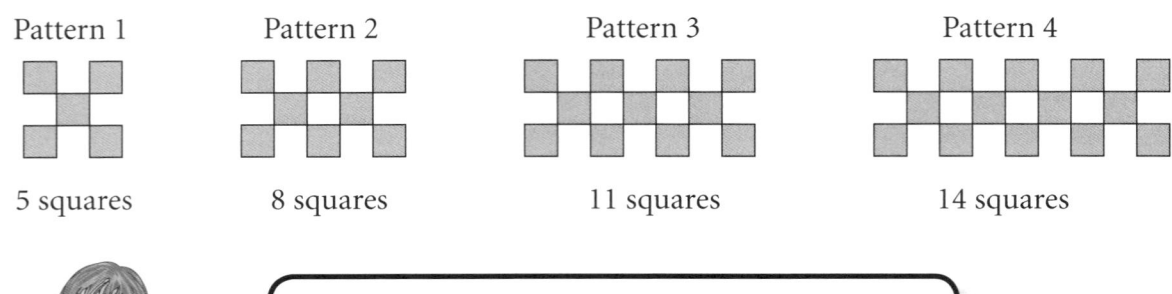

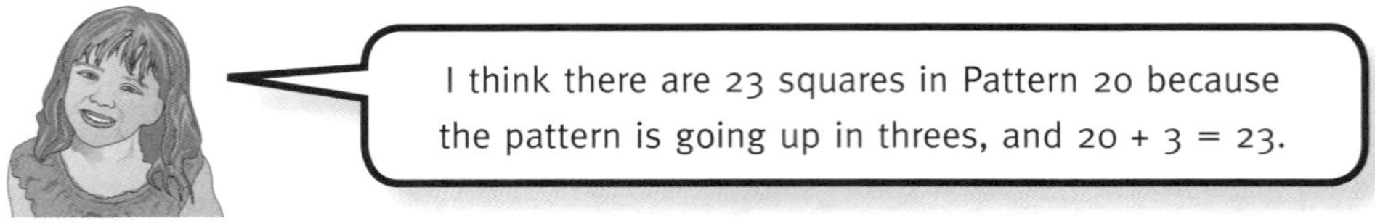

I think there are 23 squares in Pattern 20 because the pattern is going up in threes, and 20 + 3 = 23.

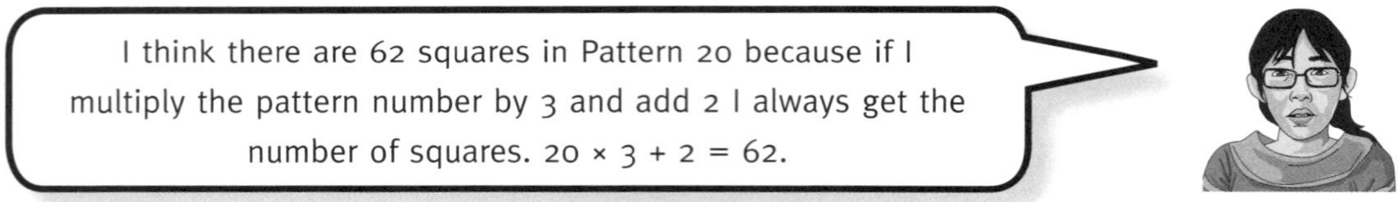

I think there are 62 squares in Pattern 20 because if I multiply the pattern number by 3 and add 2 I always get the number of squares. 20 × 3 + 2 = 62.

Who is correct? Explain your answer.

2 Sequences, expressions and formulae

Exercise 2.3 Representing simple functions

1 Copy these function machines and find the missing inputs and outputs.

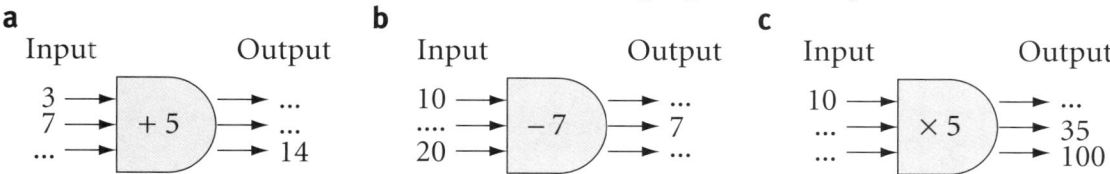

2 Copy these function machines and find the missing inputs and outputs.

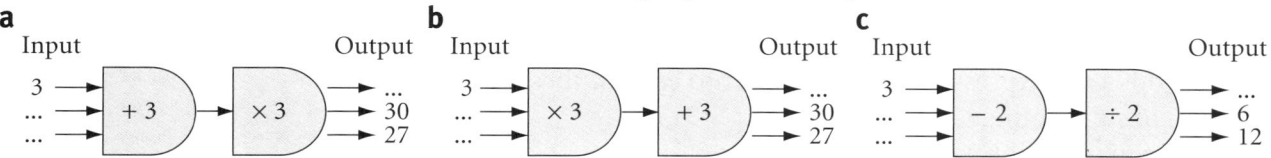

3 Work out the rule to complete these function machines.

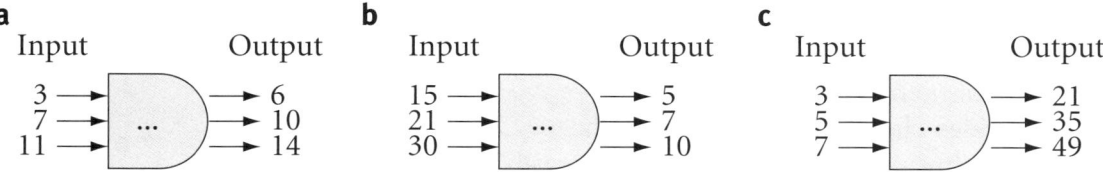

4 Copy and complete the mapping diagram below for this function machine.

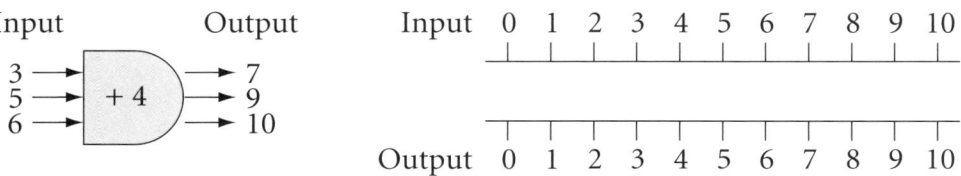

5 Jake and Hassan look at this function machine.

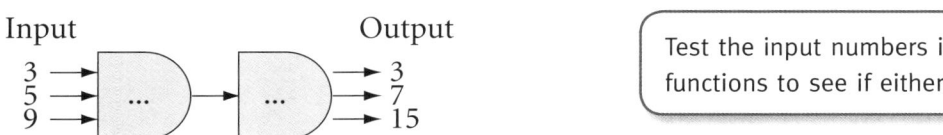

Test the input numbers in each of their functions to see if either of them is correct.

Jake says: 'I think the function is multiply by 2 then take away 3.'
Hassan says: 'I think the function is multiply by 3 then take away 3.'
Who is correct? Explain your answer.

6 Razi draws this mapping diagram and function machine of the same function.

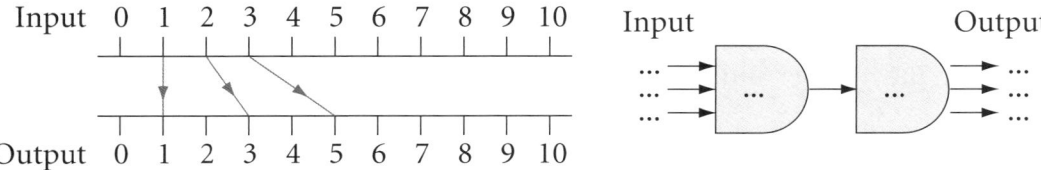

Fill in the missing numbers and write the rule in the function machine.

2 Sequences, expressions and formulae   15

Exercise 2.4 Constructing expressions

1 Shen has a box that contains t toys.
 Write an expression for the total number of toys
 he has in the box when:
   a he puts in 4 more   b he takes 2 out
   c he adds 5   d he takes out half of them.

> In each part of the question Shen starts with t toys.

2 Dafydd has a bag with s sweets in it.
 Write an expression for someone who has a bag with:
   a 2 more sweets than Dafydd   b 3 times as many sweets as Dafydd
   c 6 fewer sweets than Dafydd   d half as many sweets as Dafydd.

3 Write down an expression for the answer to each of these.
   a Ali has x paintings. He buys 2 more.
      How many paintings does he now have?
   b Hamza has t free SMS's on his mobile phone each month.
      So far this month he has used 15 SMS's.
      How many free SMS's does he have left?
   c Ibrahim is i years old and Tareq is t years old.
      What is the total of their ages?
   d Aya can store v video clips on one memory card.
      How many video clips can he store on 2 memory cards?
   e Rania is given $\$d$ for her birthday.
      She spends a quarter of the money on make-up.
      How much does she spend on make-up?

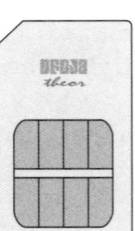

4 Nesreen thinks of a number, n.
 Write an expression for the number Nesreen gets each time.
   a She multiplies the number by 6.   b She multiplies the number by 5 then adds 1.
   c She multiplies the number by 7
      then subtracts 2.   d She divides the number by 4.
   e She divides the number by 2
      then adds 10.   f She divides the number by 5 then subtracts 3.

5 The cost of an adult meal in a fast food restaurant is $\$a$.
 The cost of a child's meal in the same restaurant is $\$c$.
 Write an expression for the total cost of meals for each group.
   a 1 adult and 1 child   b 1 adult and 3 children
   c 4 adults and 1 child   d 4 adults and 5 children

6 Fatima thinks of a number, n.
 Write an expression for the number Fatima gets each time.
   a She adds 2 to the number and then multiplies by 3.
   b She adds 2 to the number and then divides by 3.
   c She subtracts 5 from the number and then multiplies by 4.
   d She subtracts 5 from the number and then divides by 4.

> Remember to use brackets if an addition or a subtraction must be done before a multiplication or a division.

2 Sequences, expressions and formulae

7 Match each description to the correct expression.

	Description		Expression
a	Multiply x by 5 and subtract from 4.	i	$5(x + 4)$
b	Add 4 and x then multiply by 5.	ii	$4 + \frac{x}{5}$
c	Multiply x by 5 and subtract 4.	iii	$4 - 5x$
d	Multiply x by 5 and add 4.	iv	$4 + 5x$
e	Add 4 and x then divide by 5.	v	$5x - 4$
f	Divide x by 5 and add 4.	vi	$4 - \frac{x}{5}$
		vii	$\frac{x+4}{5}$

Write a description for the expression that you did not match up.

Exercise 2.5 Deriving and using formulae

1 Work out the value of each expression.
  a $a + 10$ when $a = 6$
  b $b - 3$ when $b = 120$
  c $c + z$ when $c = 3$ and $z = 17$
  d $d - y$ when $d = 40$ and $y = 15$
  e $3e$ when $e = 20$
  f $\frac{f}{5}$ when $f = 35$
  g $g + 2x$ when $g = 1$ and $x = 6$
  h $h - 4w$ when $h = 17$ and $w = 2$
  i $2i + 3v$ when $i = 3$ and $v = 2$
  j $\frac{j}{2} + u$ when $j = 30$ and $u = 3$
  k $\frac{24}{k} - 3$ when $k = 8$
  l $\frac{p+q}{3}$ when $p = 11$ and $q = 22$

2 Jana uses this formula to work out how much money her friends will collect from their sponsored walk.

Money collected = distance walked (number of km) × sponsor rate ($ per km)

How much do these friends collect?
  a Miriam walks 5 kilometres at a sponsor rate of $16 per kilometre.
  b Yara walks 8 kilometres at a sponsor rate of $18 per kilometre.

3 a Write a formula for the number of hours in any number of days, using:
  i words   **ii** letters.
  b Use your formula in part **a ii** to work out the number of hours in 4 days.

4 Use the formula $A = bh$ to work out A when: bh means $b \times h$
  a $b = 4$ and $h = 5$ **b** $b = 3$ and $h = 12$.

2 Sequences, expressions and formulae

5 Hiroto uses this formula to work out the time it should take him to travel from his house to any of his friends' houses.

$T = \dfrac{D}{S}$ where: T is the time in hours
D is the distance in kilometres
S is the average speed in kilometres per hour

$\dfrac{D}{S}$ means $D \div S$

How long does it take Hiroto to travel from his house to:
a Souta's house, 60 kilometres away, at an average speed of 20 kilometres per hour
b Hina's house, 140 kilometres away, at an average speed of 40 kilometres per hour?

6 Aqil uses this formula to work out how long different meat takes to cook.

kt means $k \times t$

$T = kt + w$ where: *T is the time required*
k is weight of meat in kilograms
t is the cooking time per kilogram
w is the extra time some meat requires.

How much time, T, does each of piece of meat require?
a 2 kg chicken, which needs 40 minutes per kg plus an extra 20 minutes
b 5 kg turkey, which needs 35 minutes per kg plus an extra 50 minutes

7 What value of x can you substitute into each of these expressions to give you the <u>same</u> answer?

$x + 12$ $4x$ $6x - 8$

8 Shira needs to hire a small car for one day.

She sees two adverts for car hire.

Shira estimates that she needs to drive 80 km.

Which car hire company should she choose?

Elite Cars
Small cars, daily rate:
($0.30 × number km driven) + $25

Cars 4 hire
Small cars, cost per day:
($0.25 × number km driven) + $35

2 Sequences, expressions and formulae

3 Place value, ordering and rounding

◆ Exercise 3.1 Understanding decimals

1 Here are some decimal numbers.

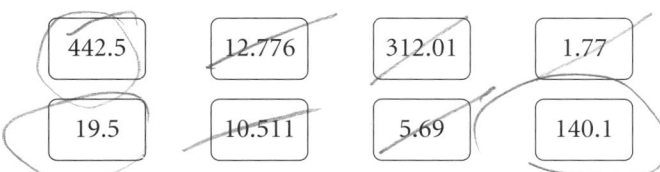

Write down all the numbers that have exactly:
a one decimal place   b two decimal places   c three decimal places.

2 Write down the value of the **bold** digit in each of these numbers.
a 11.3**7**   b **3**.908   c 2.5**9**3
d 3.0**3**1   e 1**3**6.2   f 12.564**3**

3 Maurice Greene holds the world record for the 60 m men's sprint.
His time was 6.39 seconds.
Write down the value of each of the digits described below.
a The 9 in 6.39   b The 6 in 6.39   c The 3 in 6.39

4 Theo has a dog that weighs 9 kilograms and 15 hundredths of a kilogram.
Write the weight of Theo's dog as a decimal number.

◆ Exercise 3.2 Multiplying and dividing by 10, 100 and 1000

1 Work these out.
a 28 × 10   b 400 ÷ 10   c 5.5 × 10   d 22 ÷ 10
e 0.537 × 10   f 14.73 ÷ 10   g 44 × 100   h 390 ÷ 100
i 7.1 × 100   j 24 ÷ 10   k 0.01 × 100   l 1.3 ÷ 100
m 11.5 × 1000   n 850 ÷ 1000   o 0.0337 × 100   p 2.6 ÷ 1000

2 Hannah works out 350 ÷ 10.
Then she checks her answer by working backwards.
This is what she writes.

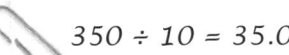

350 ÷ 10 = 35.0   Check: 35.0 × 10 = 350 ✓

Work out the answers to these questions.
Check your answers by working backwards.
a 5.1 × 10   b 0.06 × 1000   c 12.7 ÷ 10
d 18.4 ÷ 100   e 20.02 × 10

3 Write down which of × or ÷ goes in each box.
a 22 ☐ 10 = 2.2   b 17 ☐ 100 = 0.17   c 0.04 ☐ 100 = 4
d 0.9 ☐ 100 = 0.009   e 5.3 ☐ 1000 = 5300   f 0.59 ☐ 100 = 0.0059

4 Write down which number, 10, 100 or 1000, goes in each box.
a 51.3 × ☐ = 513   b 3.75 × ☐ = 37.5   c 0.0005 × ☐ = 0.05
d 1.4 ÷ ☐ = 0.014   e 180 ÷ ☐ = 0.18   f 0.1 ÷ ☐ = 0.001

5 Rocky is building a wall.
He estimates he needs 2000 bricks for the job he is doing.
The bricks are sold in packs of 100.
How many packs does he need?

6 Royston sees this poster on a fruit stall.
How much does each orange cost?

> **Oranges**
> 100 for $22.50

7 Harsha thought of a number.

> I multiplied my number by 100, and then divided the answer by 10.
> Then I multiplied this answer by 1000. My final answer was 7.

What number did Harsha first think of?

◆ Exercise 3.3 Ordering decimals

1 Write down the smaller decimal number from each pair.
  a 3.5, 9.1   b 214.92, 311.67   c 34.56, 43.652   d 638.06, 336.9   e 0.22, 0.3
  f 5.6, 5.41   g 25.67, 25.76   h 0.02, 0.013   i 0.009, 0.01   j 0.05, 0.049

2 Write the correct sign, < or >, between each pair of numbers.
  a 2.05 ☐ 2.24   b 8.55 ☐ 8.41   c 0.48 ☐ 0.51   d 18.05 ☐ 18.02
  e 8.2 ☐ 8.01   f 2.18 ☐ 2.205   g 0.072 ☐ 0.02   h 28.882 ☐ 28.88

3 Write the decimal numbers in each list in order of size. Start with the smallest.
  a 4.46, 2.66, 4.41, 4.49   b 0.71, 0.52, 0.77, 0.59   c 6.09, 6.92, 6.9, 6.97
  d 5.212, 5.2, 5.219, 5.199   e 42.449, 42.42, 42.441, 42.4   f 9.09, 9.7, 9.901, 9.04, 9.99

4 The table shows six of the fastest times for the men's 100 m sprint.
Who is the third fastest runner in this list?
Explain how you worked out your answer.

Name	Country	Time (seconds)
Donovan Bailey	Canada	9.84
Nesta Carter	Jamaica	9.78
Tyson Gay	USA	9.69
Asafa Powell	Jamaica	9.72
Usain Bolt	Jamaica	9.58
Maurice Greene	USA	9.79

5 Zack has put these decimal number cards in order of size, starting with the smallest.

  [6.46]   [6.▓▓▓]   [6.471]

He has spilt coffee on the middle card.
Write down three possible numbers that could be on the middle card.

Exercise 3.4 Rounding

1. Round each number to the nearest 10.
   a 77   b 22   c 383
   d 227   e 4375   f 6203

2. Round each number to the nearest 100.
   a 538   b 480   c 6395
   d 5703   e 51 362 f 55

3. Round each number to the nearest 1000.
   a 2300   b 6250   c 8307
   d 2090   e 56 792 f 690

4. Is Dakarai correct?

    If I round 706 to the nearest 10 and to the nearest 100, I get the same answer!

   Explain your answer.

5. Round each decimal measurement to the nearest whole number.
   a 9.4 m   b 36.7 mm   c 377.17 km
   d 302.801 kg   e 39.7 cm

6. Round each number to one decimal place.
   a 0.11   b 5.55   c 6.78
   d 12.292   e 98.765 f 0.0901

7. Jake, Maha and Ahmed are rounding 70.952 to one decimal place.

   That rounds up to 70.9.

   That rounds up to 71.

   That rounds up to 71.0.

   Who is correct? Explain your answer.

Exercise 3.5 Adding and subtracting decimals

1 Use a mental method to work these out.
   a 5.5 + 2.3   b 12.3 + 5.5   c 8.7 + 6.5
   d 8.8 − 3.4   e 18.6 − 7.4   f 12.3 − 5.5

2 Work these out by rounding one of the numbers to a whole number.
   Remember to reverse the rounding when you write down your answer.
   a 5.9 + 3.3   b 8.7 + 8.9   c 5.8 + 6.3
   d 7.3 − 2.9   e 9.7 − 4.6   f 13.5 − 8.8

3 Use a written method to work these out.
   a 7.67 + 0.15   b 7.77 + 5.55   c 23.4 + 6.78   d 45.67 + 76.5
   e 8.64 − 6.42   f 9.75 − 7.95   g 23.4 − 4.32   h 77.7 − 38.66

4 At the cinema, Bijoux spends $1.50 on a ticket, $1.75 on food and $0.85 on a drink.
   a How much does she spend altogether?
   Bijoux pays with a $5 note.
   b How much change does she receive?

5 Dewain repairs fibreglass boats.
   He has four pieces of fibreglass cloth that are 0.6 m, 1.35 m, 1.6 m and 3 m long.
   a What is the total length of the four pieces?
   Dewain needs 8 m of fibreglass cloth altogether.
   b How much more fibreglass cloth does he need to buy?

6 Lesia records the weight of her puppy at the start and end of every month.
   Here are her records for April and May.

Date	Weight (kg)	Date	Weight (kg)
Start of April	6.43	End of April	7.22
Start of May	7.22	End of May	8.05

   a During which month, April or May, did the puppy gain more weight?
   During June the puppy gets 0.93 kg heavier.
   b How much does the puppy weigh at the end of June?

7 Work out the missing digits in these calculations.

   a   ☐ 7 . ☐ 2
     + 2 ☐ . 5 ☐
       6 6 . 1 5

   b   ☐ 4 . 5 6
      − 2 ☐ . 5 ☐
        5 5 . ☐ 7

Exercise 3.6 Multiplying decimals

1 Use a mental method to work these out.
   a 0.3 × 2   b 0.2 × 4   c 0.4 × 6   d 5 × 0.6   e 7 × 0.7   f 0.8 × 6

2 Use a written method to work these out.
   a 3 × 3.6   b 7 × 3.6   c 3.6 × 9   d 4 × 4.8   e 7 × 4.8   f 4.8 × 9

3 Use a written method to work these out.
   a 3 × 3.69   b 7 × 3.69   c 3.69 × 9   d 4 × 4.82   e 7 × 4.82   f 4.82 × 9

4 Use the numbers from the box to complete these calculations. You can only use each number once. You should have no numbers left at the end.

   0.4   0.5   0.6   2   4   6   3.8

   a 0.2 × 3 = ☐
   b 0.6 × ☐ = 2.4
   c ☐ × 9 = 4.5
   d 6.3 × ☐ = 37.8
   e 7.6 × 0.5 = ☐
   f ☐ × 5 = ☐

Exercise 3.7 Dividing decimals

1 Work these out.
   a 9.6 ÷ 3   b 8.2 ÷ 2   c 2.8 ÷ 7   d 6.4 ÷ 8   e 7.2 ÷ 3   f 8.4 ÷ 6

2 Work these out.
   a 9.36 ÷ 3   b 4.68 ÷ 2   c 3.03 ÷ 3   d 5.15 ÷ 5   e 8.13 ÷ 3   f 7.86 ÷ 6

3 Work these out.
   a 5.78 ÷ 2   b 9.51 ÷ 3   c 3.04 ÷ 4   d 19.15 ÷ 5   e 23.64 ÷ 6   f 21.42 ÷ 7

4 Kai pays $7.45 for 5 bags of cement. How much does one bag of cement cost?

5 Rosi pays $7.56 for 6 bags of beads. How much does one bag of beads cost?

6 Copy and complete these divisions.

   a 2) 8 . ☐ ¹6   with quotient ☐ . 2 ☐
   b 3) ☐ . ¹7 ☐   with quotient 1 . ☐ 7
   c ☐) 3 3 . ³5 ☐   with quotient 5 . ☐ 9

3 Place value, ordering and rounding

 **Exercise 3.8 Estimating and approximating**

1 Work out an estimate for each of these.
  a 39 + 73   b 91 − 49   c 52 × 19   d 78 ÷ 18   e 488 + 607   f 412 × 29

2 For each of the following:
  i work out an estimate of the answer
  ii work out the correct answer, correct to one decimal place
  iii compare your estimate with the accurate answer to check that your answer is correct.

  a $\dfrac{289 + 401}{14}$ b $\dfrac{712.2 - 86.6}{28.92}$ c $\dfrac{78.3 \times 8}{40.5}$ d $\dfrac{6 \times 47.95}{29.2}$

3 For each of the following:
  i work out the accurate answer
  ii use an inverse operation to check your answer.
  a 237.7 + 62.5   b 41.28 − 39.93   c 5 × 22.8   d 51.42 ÷ 3

 4 This is part of Adrian's homework.

> *Question* Mandy buys some chocolate in Switzerland for 8 CHF when the exchange rate is 1 CHF = $1.15. How much does the chocolate cost, in dollars?
>
> *Answer* 8 = 9.2, the chocolate cost $9.2
> Check: 9.2 ÷ 8 = 1.15

Write down the things that are missing from Adrian's solution.

In questions 5, 6 and 7:
  i   solve the problem
  ii explain what you have worked out
  iii check your answer by estimation or using an inverse operation.
  iv make sure your workings are clear and neatly presented.

 5 Shari is training for a 10-kilometre race.
  On Tuesday she runs 6.6 km and on Thursday she runs 8.2 km.
  a What is the total distance she has run?
  Shari wants to run 30 km each week.
  b How much further does she have to run this week?

6 Vea is a carpenter. He charges $18 per hour.
  a Vea takes 8.5 hours to do a job on Monday.
     How much does he charge for this job?
  b For his next job, Vea charges a total of $243.
     How long did this job take him?

 7 Hewi is building a brick wall.
  He needs 65 bricks for each row of the wall.
  The wall must be 42 rows high.
  Bricks are delivered in pallets of 500.
  How many pallets does Hewi need?

4 Length, mass and capacity

Exercise 4.1 Knowing metric units

1 Which of **A**, **B**, **C** or **D** shows the correct method to convert these units?
Write the letter.

a	km to m	A: × 100	B: ÷ 100	C: × 1000	D: ÷ 1000
b	g to kg	A: × 100	B: ÷ 100	C: × 1000	D: ÷ 1000
c	mm to m	A: × 100	B: ÷ 100	C: × 1000	D: ÷ 1000
d	cm to m	A: × 100	B: ÷ 100	C: × 1000	D: ÷ 1000

2 Convert these lengths into the units shown.

a 9 m = □ cm **b** 8.1 km = □ m **c** 50 mm = □ cm
d 7000 m = □ km **e** 220 cm = □ m **f** 75 mm = □ cm
g 86 cm = □ mm **h** 6.6 m = □ cm **i** 455 m = □ km

3 Convert these masses into the units shown.

a 7.5 t = □ kg **b** 975 g = □ kg **c** 3000 kg = □ t
d 9900 g = □ kg **e** 0.2 kg = □ t **f** 6 kg = □ g

4 Convert these capacities into the units shown.

a 2000 ml = □ l **b** 6 l = □ ml **c** 8.8 l = □ ml
d 5500 ml = □ l **e** 0.2 l = □ ml **f** 990 ml = □ l

5 Use the items from the box to complete these conversions.
You should not have any spare items.

÷ 55 550 1000 mm cm m

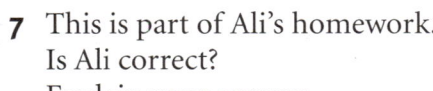

a 5.5 t × □ = 5500 kg **b** 5.5 □ × 10 = 55 mm **c** 55 mm □ 10 = 5.5 cm
d 0.55 m × 100 = □ cm **e** □ ml ÷ 1000 = 0.55 l **f** 850 □ ÷ 1000 = 0.85 □

6 Write these decimal measurements in order of size.
Start with the smallest.

a 27 cm, 0.3 m, 280 mm **b** 7.2 l, 635 ml, 0.6 l
c 0.555 kg, 88 g, 0.06 kg **d** 3.1 km, 3.095 km, 3250 m

7 This is part of Ali's homework.
Is Ali correct?
Explain your answer.

Question Convert 65 km into metres.
Solution 65 ÷ 1000 = 0.065 m

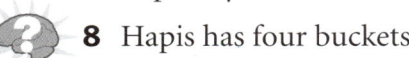

8 Hapis has four buckets.

The buckets hold 4700 ml, 4.8 l, 3880 ml and 4.75 l.
Hapis wants to use the bucket that holds the closest to 5 litres.
Which bucket should he use? Show your working.

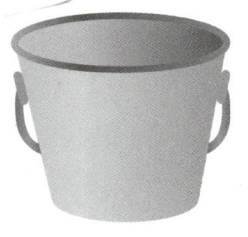

4700 ml 4.8 l 3880 ml 4.75 l

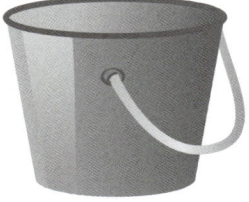

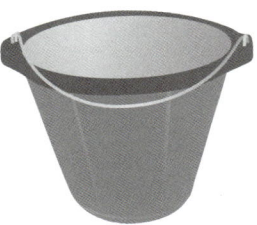

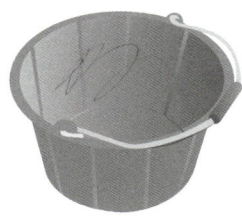

9 What are the two possible lengths Maha could be thinking of?

> I am thinking of a length in centimetres.
> My length is a whole number of centimetres.
> It is smaller than 0.673 m but larger than 659 mm.

◆ Exercise 4.2 Choosing suitable units

1 Which metric units would you use to measure:
   a the capacity of a bucket   **b** the mass of an orange
   c the mass of a lorry   **d** the width of this maths book
   e the length of a finger   **f** the mass of a car tyre
   g the capacity of a spoon   **h** the length of a rugby pitch?

2 Which measurement, **W**, **X** or **Y**, is most likely to be correct for each object? Write the letter.
   a The length of a dog   **W:** 50 mm   **X:** 50 cm   **Y:** 50 m
   b The mass of a child   **W:** 33 g   **X:** 330 g   **Y:** 33 kg
   c The capacity of a cup   **W:** 30 ml   **X:** 300 ml   **Y:** 3 l
   d The height of a skyscraper **W:** 200 mm   **X:** 200 cm   **Y:** 200 m
   e The mass of a car   **W:** 900 g   **X:** 900 kg   **Y:** 900 t

3 Milton has a pet kitten. He estimates that it weighs 250 kg.
   Does this estimate make sense? Give a reason for your answer.

4 Milli has a new desk. She estimates that the length of the desk is 120 cm.
   Does this estimate make sense? Give a reason for your answer.

4 Length, mass and capacity

Exercise 4.3 Reading scales

1 Write down the value shown on each of these scales.
Remember to include the correct units.

a m 21 22
b cm 30 40 50
c mm 7 8 9

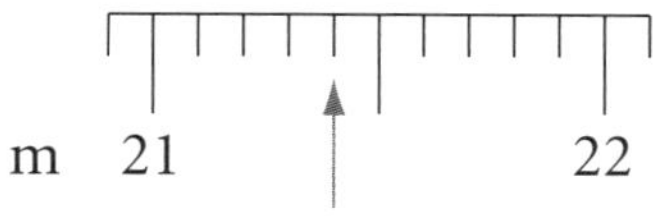

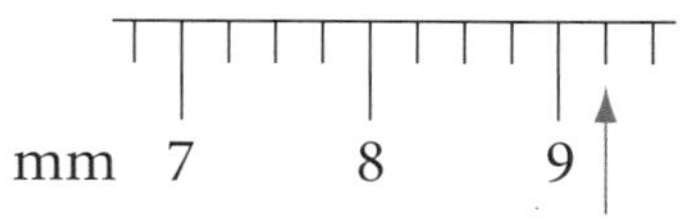

d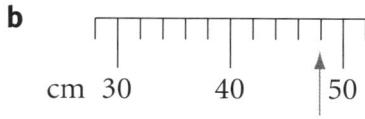
e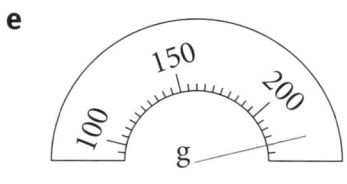
f litres

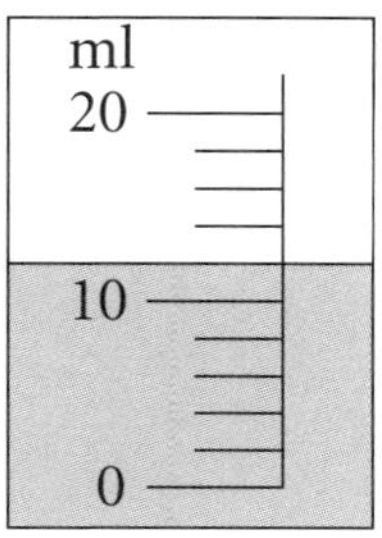

2 Dakarai says that this scale shows a mass of 19.1 g.
Is he correct?
Explain your answer.

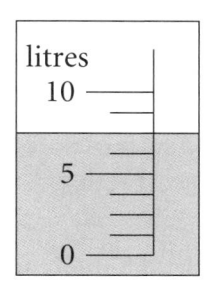

3 Estimate the reading on each of these scales.

a m 7 8
b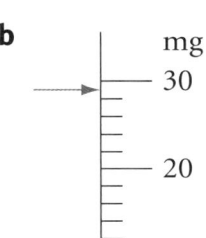
c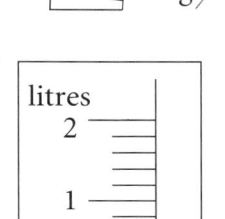
d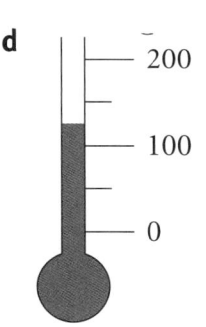

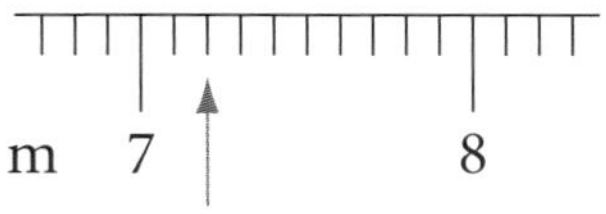

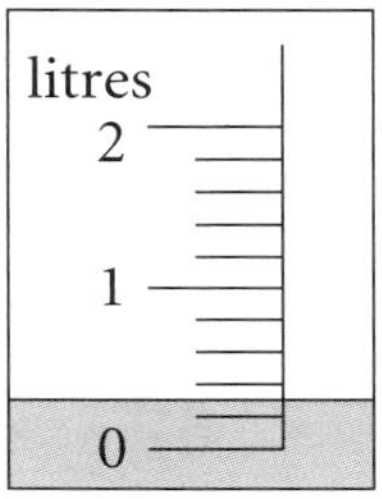

4 Shen is comparing the temperatures of two liquids in an experiment.
This is his diagram, from his notes.

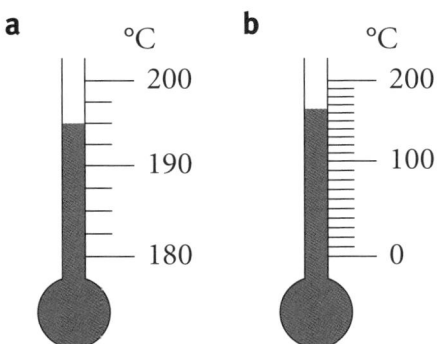

What is the difference in the readings of the two thermometers?

4 Length, mass and capacity

5 Angles

Exercise 5.1 Labelling and estimating angles

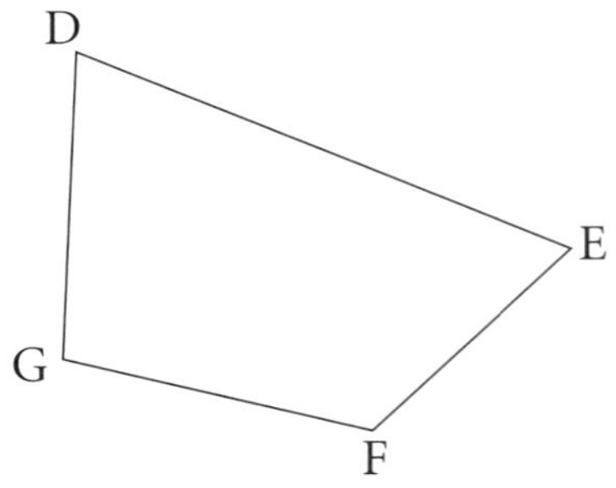

1 **a** Sketch this quadrilateral and mark angle EFG.
   b Write down a three-letter name for the angle opposite angle EFG.

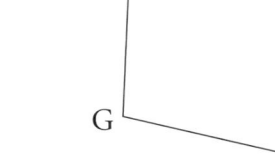

2 Here are the sizes of some angles. Say whether each is acute, obtuse or reflex.
   a 210°   **b** 120°   **c** 31°   **d** 301°   **e** 103°

3 Look at each statement and write down whether it it:
   i always true   **ii** sometimes true   **iii** never true.
   a An angle that is less than 75° is acute.
   b An angle that is bigger than 100° is obtuse.
   c An angle that is bigger than 330° is reflex.
   d An angle that is less than 330° is reflex.
   e An angle half the size of a reflex angle is an obtuse angle.

4 Here are five angles. Estimate the size of each one.

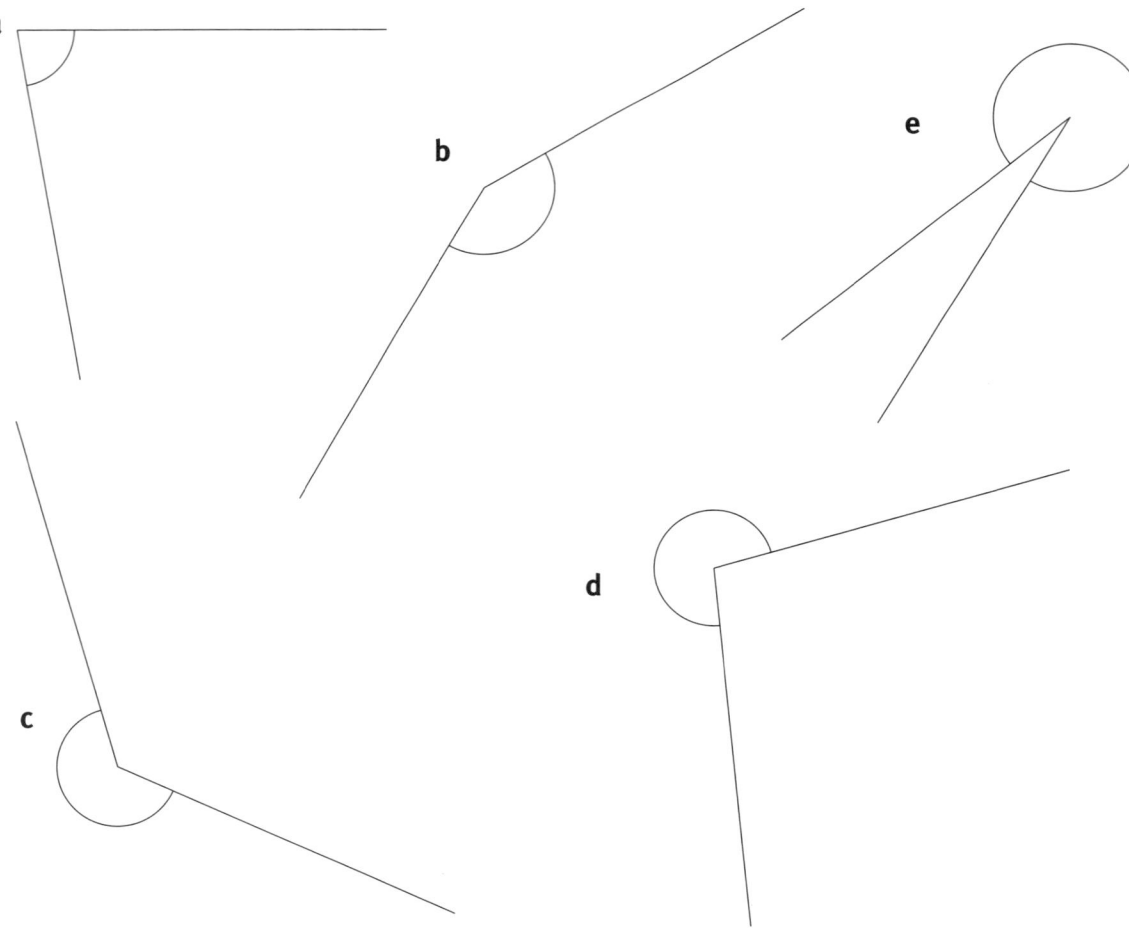

5 Write down the size of each of these angles.
  a angle ADB
  b reflex angle ADB
  c reflex angle BDC
  d reflex angle ADC

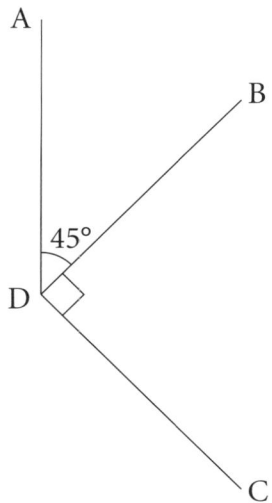

Not drawn accurately

6 Angle ABC is an acute angle.

Find examples of the following.
  a an obtuse angle
  b a reflex angle that is more than three right angles
  c a reflex angle that is less than three right angles

Exercise 5.2 Drawing and measuring angles

1 i Estimate the size of each angle below.   **ii** Measure each angle.

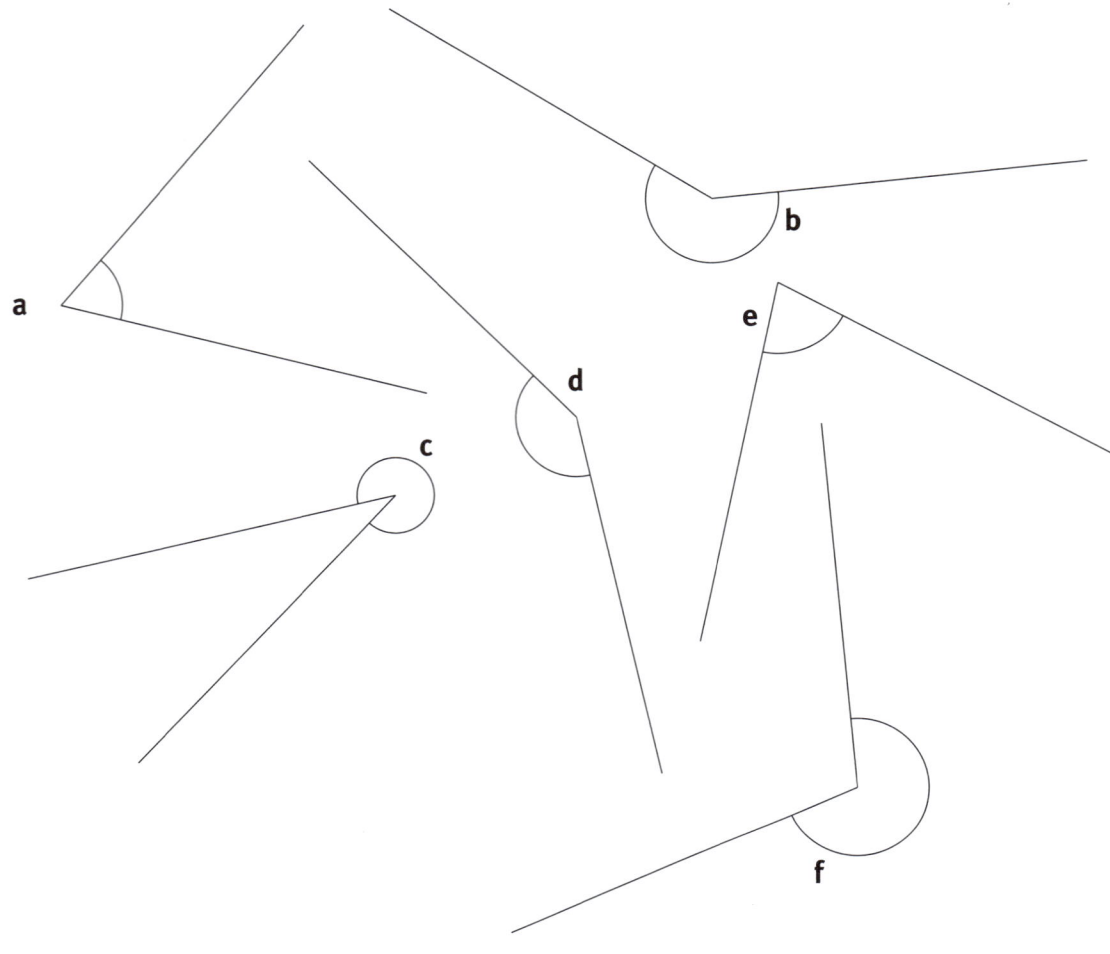

2 Draw the following angles.
   a 46°   **b** 146°   **c** 246°   **d** 346°   **e** 109°   **f** 296°

3 Measure the reflex angle at each vertex of this triangle.

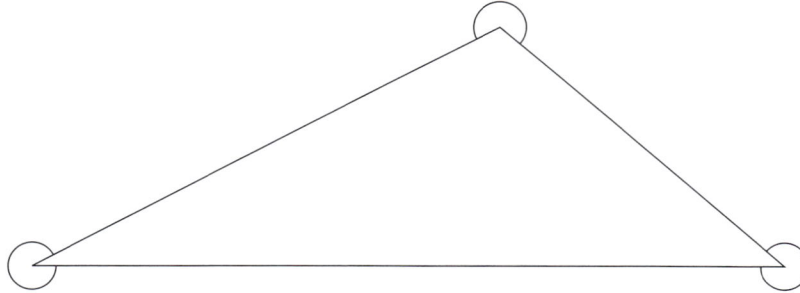

5 Angles

4 Measure the angles in this diagram.

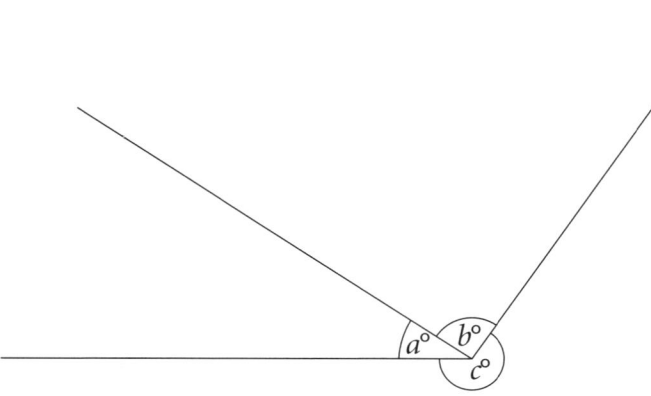

5 a Measure the angles labelled *x*, *y* and *z*.

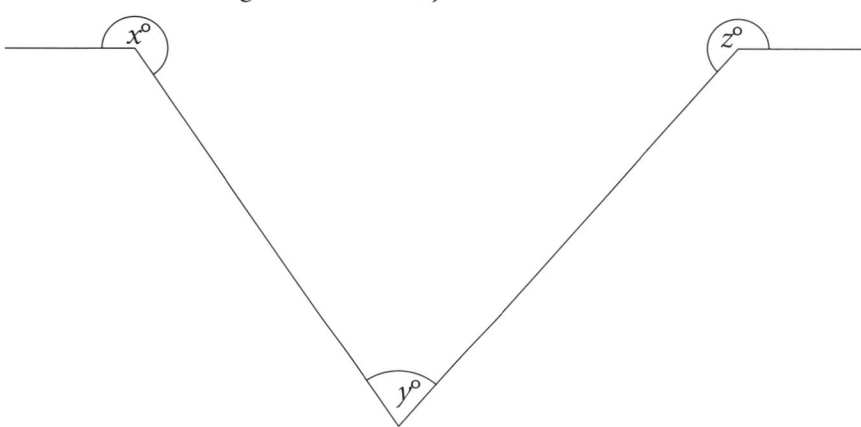

b $x° + y° + z° = 540°$.

Use this fact to check your measurements.

6 The reflex angle at each vertex of a triangle is 300°.
What is the special name for this triangle?

Exercise 5.3 Calculating angles

1 Calculate the values of the letters in these angles.

a

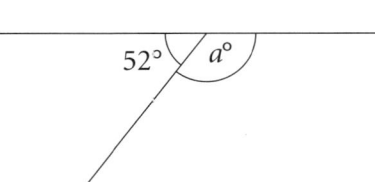

b

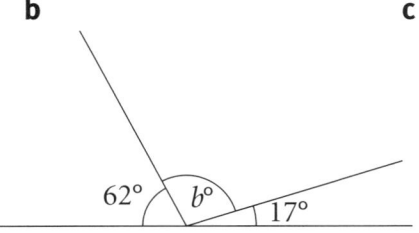

c

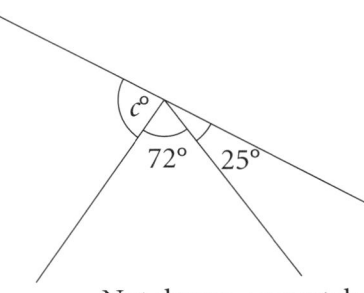

Not drawn accurately

5 Angles

2 Calculate the sizes of the lettered angles.

a 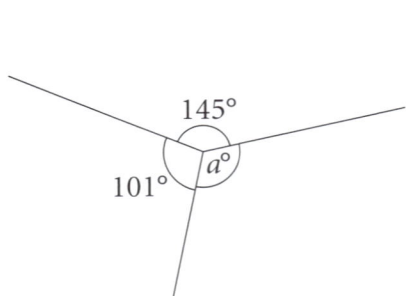 b c

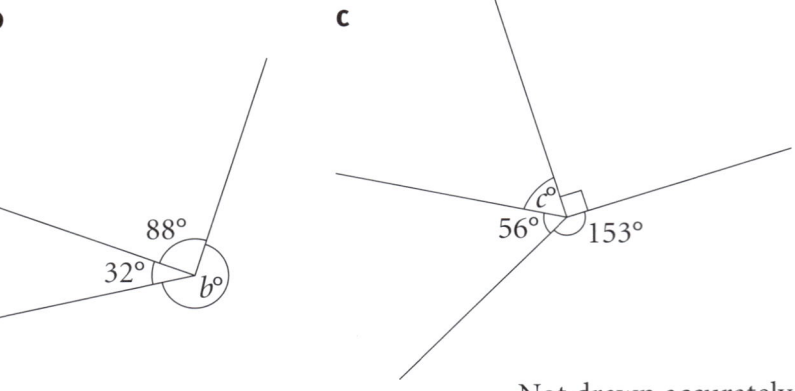

Not drawn accurately

3 Each part gives two angles of a triangle. Calculate the third angle in each case.
 a 42° and 78° b 37° and 15° c 75° and 75° d 153° and 14°

4 Calculate the size of the angle marked with a letter in each of these diagrams.

a b c

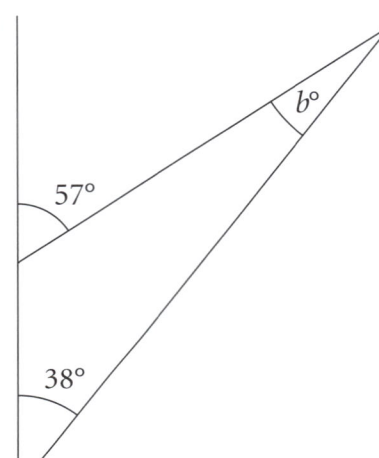
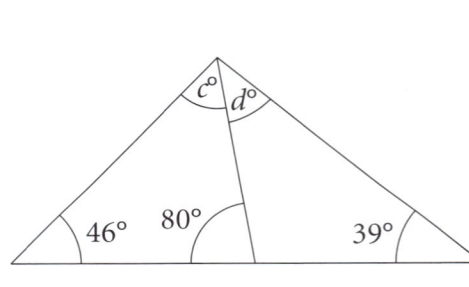

Not drawn accurately

5 All the angles of a triangle are whole numbers. All the angles are different. What is the largest possible size of the biggest angle?

6 Each part gives three angles of a quadrilateral. Calculate the fourth angle in each case.
 a 65°, 75° and 85°   b 135°, 98° and 71°   c 84°, 84° and 111°

7 Three of the angles of a quadrilateral are each 105°. Calculate the fourth angle.

8 Calculate the sizes of the lettered angles.

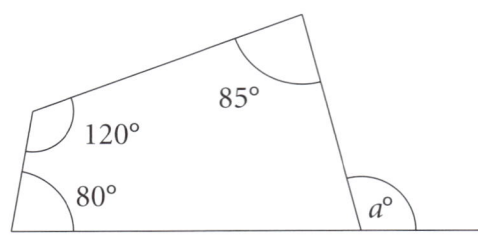

Not drawn accurately

5 Angles

9 Raoul cuts one corner from an equilateral triangle. What can you say about the values of *a* and *b*?

10 Calculate the size of angle:
   a angle BDE   **b** angle CBD   **c** angle ACE

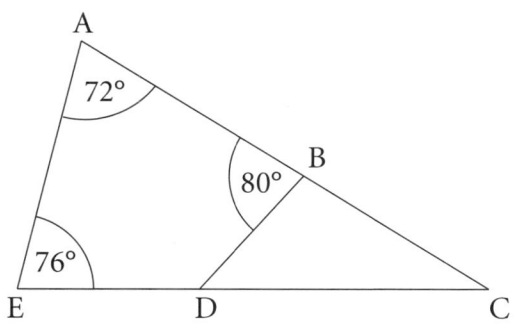

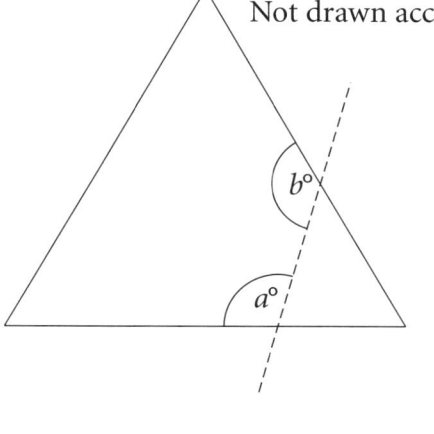
Not drawn accurately

Not drawn accurately

◆ Exercise 5.4 Solving angle problems

1 The diagram shows three straight lines crossing at one point. Calculate *a*, *b* and *c*.

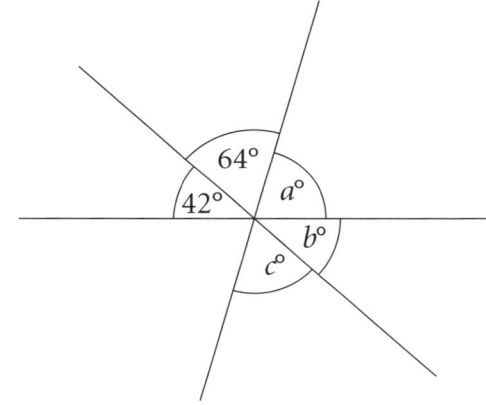

Not drawn accurately

2 AB and CD are perpendicular lines.

Calculate the following angles, giving a reason for your answer in each case.
   a angle BGF   **b** angle EGC   **c** angle AGE

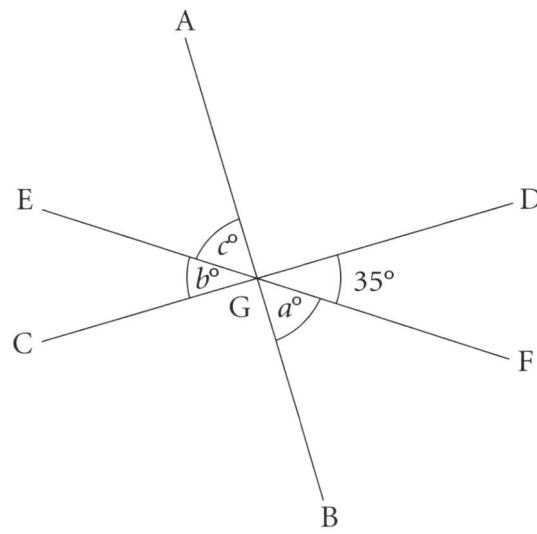

Not drawn accurately

5 Angles   33

3 Lines PR and SU are parallel.
   Find the sizes of the following angles.
   a angle RQW   **b** angle VTS   **c** angle VTU

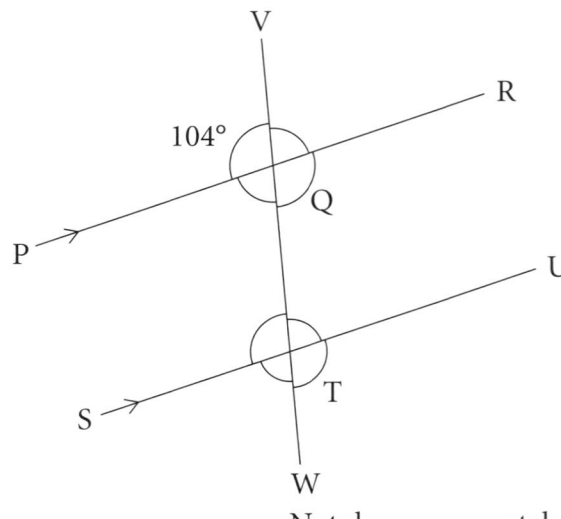
Not drawn accurately

4 Two angles of a triangle are 128° and 26°.
  Explain why the triangle must be isosceles.

5 One angle of an isosceles triangle is 38°.
  What could the other angles be?

6 AB, AC and AD are both the same length.
  Calculate the size of each of these angles.
   a angle ABC   **b** angle ADC   **c** angle BCD

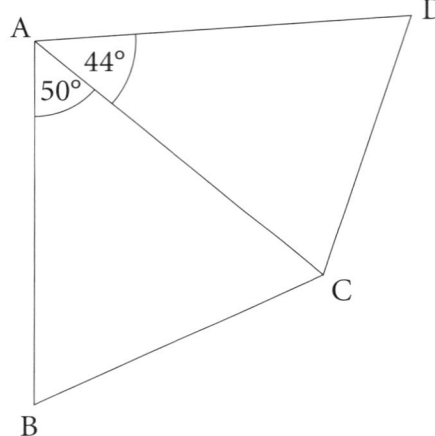
Not drawn accurately

7 Calculate angles *a*, *b*, *c* and *d*.

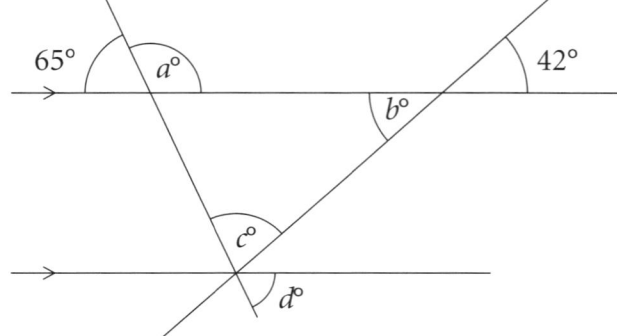

Not drawn accurately

34   **5** Angles

6 Planning and collecting data

◆ Exercise 6.1 Planning to collect data

1 In a survey, which units from the box would you use to measure each quantity?

   seconds minutes hours
   km kg cm cl l

   a The time it takes to for a person to count to 10
   b The distance a person can walk in 2 hours
   c The time it takes to read this entire book

2 Where would you get the data to help you answer these questions?
   a Which is the second longest river in the world?
   b How many people work in your village or town?
   c How many pieces of meat does your local shop sell every day?
   d How many students were absent from school last week?

3 Which sort of data, primary or secondary, would you collect to answer these questions?
   a What is the favourite colour of the students in your class?
   b Which country has the fastest-growing population?
   c How much money did the top five golfers earn last year?
   d Where would your family members most like to go on holiday?

4 When you collect primary data you can either carry out a survey (S) and ask people questions or carry out an experiment (E) and record the results.
   For each of the following questions, decide whether you should carry out a survey or an experiment. Write S or E for each answer.
   a How often do the members of your family visit the dentist?
   b What is the favourite pet of students in your class?
   c How many times does a dice land on '6' when it is rolled 60 times?
   d How many of your friends are left-handed?
   e How many of your friends can hit the '20' sector in a dartboard with one throw of a dart?

 5 Umi wants to know how many of her family like vegetables. She only asks the adults.
   Will the results of her survey give a fair result?
   Give a reason for your answer.

 6 Samir wants to know if there are enough parking spaces at a busy shopping centre.
   He asks car drivers who are waiting to park at the shopping centre on a Saturday morning.
   Will the results of his survey give a fair result?
   Give a reason for your answer.

 7 Basir want to find out what people's favourite sports are.
   Every evening for one week he stands at the entrance of a busy shopping centre.
   He stops people as they go into the centre and asks them to name their favourite sports.
   Will the results of his survey give a fair result?
   Give a reason for your answer.

6 Planning and collecting data 35

Exercise 6.2 Collecting data

1 Danny asks people who live in his street about the local sports centre.
These are four of the questions he writes.

> 1 What is your name? ....
> 2 What is your date of birth? ....
> 3 Do you agree that the local sports centre is useless?
>   ☐ strongly agree   ☐ agree   ☐ not sure
> 4 How many times did you visit the local sports centre last month?
>   ☐ 0 times   ☐ 1–3 times
>   ☐ 3–5 times   ☐ more than 10 times

a Explain why each question is unsuitable.
b Re-write questions 2, 3 and 4 to make them suitable for Danny's questionnaire.

2 Siobhan asks people who live in her street about the local sports centre.
These are two of the questions she asks.

> 1 How often do you go to the local sports centre?
>   ☐ very often   ☐ often   ☐ not very often
> 2 How many times in one month do you usually go to the local sports centre?
>   ☐ 0 times   ☐ 1–3 times   ☐ 4–6 times   ☐ 7 or more times

a Give one reason why question 1 is unsuitable.
b Give two reasons why question 2 is suitable.

3 Kimberly is carrying out a survey on the number of hours students in her school spend doing homework each week.
This is one of her questions.
Design a response section for Kimberly's question.

> How many hours, on average, do you spend doing homework each week?

4 Liam is carrying out a survey to find students' favourite subjects in school.
This is one of his questions.
Design a response section for his question.

> What is your favourite subject in school?

6 Planning and collecting data

Exercise 6.3 Using frequency tables

1 Twenty students were asked to choose their favourite pet out of rabbit (R), dog (D), cat (C), horse (H) or other (O). The results are listed below.

| R | D | D | H | C | D | R | D | R | D |
| C | O | O | R | O | C | D | R | O | D |

a Copy and complete the data collection sheet to show this information.

Favourite pet	Rabbit (R)	Dog (D)	Cat (C)	Horse (H)	Other (O)

b Which pet was the most popular?

2 In a survey, students observed the first 10 cars that passed the school gate. They wrote down the number of passengers (not including the driver) in each car.
They did this at 9 am, 11 am and 1 pm.
Here are the results of the survey.
9 am: 2, 4, 3, 1, 4, 1, 2, 3, 3, 4
11 am: 2, 0, 3, 4, 0, 0, 0, 1, 2, 4
1 pm: 4, 0, 2, 4, 2, 1, 1, 1, 1, 0
Copy and complete the data collection sheet to show the information above.

		Time		
		9 am	11 am	1 pm
Number of passengers	0			
	1			
	2			
	3			
	4			

3 Thirty adults were asked to choose their favourite vegetable out of potato (P), chickpeas (C), beans (B), spinach (S), or other (O). The results are below.

B	B	C	B	P	P	B	S	P	S
P	C	P	O	S	P	P	B	B	P
S	S	P	S	B	B	P	O	P	O

a Copy and complete the frequency table to show this information.

Vegetable	Tally	Frequency
potato (P)		
chickpeas (C)		
beans (B)		
spinach (S)		
other (O)		
Total:		

b What was the most popular vegetable?

6 Planning and collecting data

4 Some people were asked to choose their favourite fruit out of apple (A), pineapple (P), banana (B), melon (M) and orange (O). The results are below.

P	P	B	O	O	O	B	O	P	A	M	P
B	O	A	M	P	O	P	A	B	P	P	M

  a Draw a frequency table to show this information.
  b What is the most popular fruit?
  c How many people were asked?

5 Mr Chamberlain gave his class a multiplication test.
The test was marked out of 40.
Here are the students' scores.

12	19	27	20	25	40	16	20	12	22	22	24	40	30
5	35	16	31	4	29	18	8	16	23	34	39	19	28

  a Copy and complete the grouped frequency table.

Score	Tally	Frequency
1–10		
11–20		
21–30		
31–40		
Total:		

  b How many students are there in Mr Chamberlain's class?
  c How many students got more than half the questions correct?
     Explain how you worked out your answer.

6 Jimmi has a 20-sided dice marked with the numbers 1 to 20.
He throws the dice 40 times and records the score each time.
These are his results.

1	11	15	19	4	19	15	20	13	17
5	9	1	6	6	1	3	16	17	8
20	12	15	2	8	11	12	14	2	2
9	2	18	7	10	20	4	19	5	6

  a Draw a grouped frequency table to show this information.
     Use the groups 1–5, 6–10, 11–15 and 16–20.
  b Do you think the dice Jimmi is using is fair? Explain your answer.

7 Fractions

✦ Exercise 7.1 Simplifying fractions

1 Copy and complete these equivalent fractions.

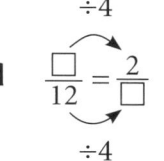

a $\dfrac{6}{10} = \dfrac{\square}{5}$ (÷2)   b $\dfrac{6}{9} = \dfrac{\square}{\square}$ (÷3)   c $\dfrac{15}{25} = \dfrac{\square}{\square}$ (÷5)   d $\dfrac{\square}{12} = \dfrac{2}{\square}$ (÷4)   e $\dfrac{16}{\square} = \dfrac{8}{11}$ (÷□)

2 Write each fraction in its simplest form.

a $\dfrac{2}{12}$ b $\dfrac{8}{16}$ c $\dfrac{4}{12}$ d $\dfrac{25}{30}$ e $\dfrac{28}{35}$

3 Write each fraction in its lowest terms.

a $\dfrac{9}{18}$ b $\dfrac{20}{24}$ c $\dfrac{15}{21}$ d $\dfrac{26}{39}$ e $\dfrac{16}{24}$

4 Copy this spider diagram.
Complete the equivalent fractions.

Centre: $\dfrac{3}{4}$

Surrounding: $\dfrac{21}{\square}$, $\dfrac{\square}{8}$, $\dfrac{\square}{20}$, $\dfrac{18}{\square}$, $\dfrac{\square}{16}$, $\dfrac{9}{\square}$

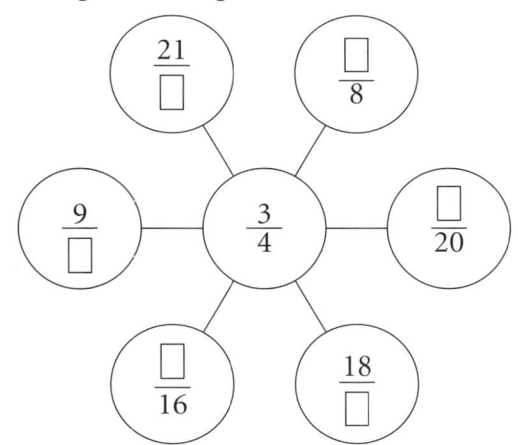

5 Eleri has these five fraction cards.

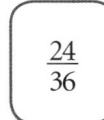

$\dfrac{24}{36}$ $\dfrac{18}{27}$ $\dfrac{14}{21}$ $\dfrac{10}{16}$ $\dfrac{12}{18}$

   a Which card is different from the rest?
   b Explain your answer.

6 What fraction is Dakarai thinking of?

> I am thinking of a fraction that is equivalent to $\dfrac{3}{7}$.
> The numerator is bigger than 25.
> The denominator is smaller than 70.

Exercise 7.2 Recognising equivalent fractions, decimals and percentages

1. Write the following decimal numbers as fractions.
   Give your answers in their simplest form.
   a 0.1   b 0.7   c 0.4   d 0.8   e 0.5
   f 0.19   g 0.32   h 0.64   i 0.09   j 0.06
   k 0.247   l 0.255   m 0.342   n 0.062   o 0.008

2. Write the following percentages as fractions.
   a 3%   b 11%   c 76%   d 53%   e 5%

3. Use numbers from the box to complete these.
   You can only use each number once.
   You should have no numbers left at the end.

   $\frac{4}{5}$ 70% $\frac{1}{5}$ 50%   0.75   0.2 $\frac{1}{4}$

   a 0.25 = ☐   b $\frac{1}{2}$ = ☐   c ☐ = 80%
   d 0.7 = ☐   e 75% = ☐   f ☐ = ☐

4. Pick the correct equaivalent fraction, A, B or C, for each of these.
   a 30% = ☐   A: 0.03   B: $\frac{3}{5}$ C: 0.3
   b 0.6 = ☐   A: $\frac{3}{5}$ B: 6%   C: $\frac{6}{100}$
   c $\frac{2}{5}$ = ☐   A: 20%   B: 0.02   C: 0.4

5. At an athletics competition, 20% of the spectators were children.
   a What fraction of the spectators were children?
   b What percentage of the spectators were not children?
   c What fraction of the spectators were not children?

6. Femke buys a pack of turkey sausages.
   This is the list of ingredients on the back
   of the pack.
   What fraction of the ingredients are not turkey?

   Premium sausages
   Ingredients: turkey 80%, rusk 8%, cranberry 5%, other ingredients 7%

7. In a cricket match, Ramesh scored $\frac{3}{10}$ of the runs for his team.
   a What percentage of the runs did Ramesh not get?
   b Explain why it is not possible to work out the number of runs Ramesh scored.
   c At the cricket match, $\frac{2}{5}$ of the spectators were supporting Pakistan.
      What percentage of the spectators were not supporting Pakistan?

Exercise 7.3 Comparing fractions

1 a Copy the number line. 0 1

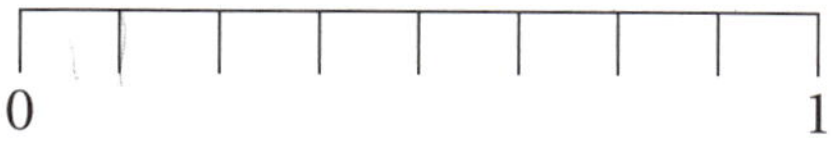

Write the fractions $\frac{1}{4}$ and $\frac{3}{8}$ in the correct positions on your number line.

b Which fraction is the larger?

2 a Copy the number line. 0 1

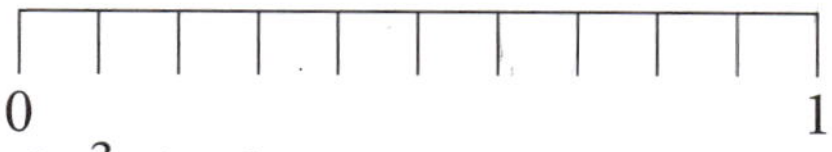

Write the fractions $\frac{2}{5}$ and $\frac{3}{10}$ in the correct positions on your number line.

b Which fraction is the larger?

3 In each part of this question:
  i copy the shapes
  ii on your copy, shade in the fraction shown next to each shape
  iii write down which is the smaller of the two fractions.

a $\frac{1}{4}$ $\frac{1}{8}$

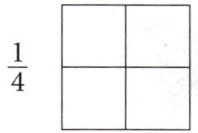

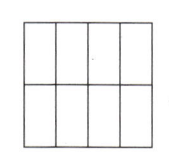

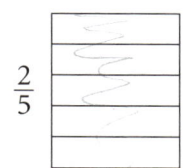

b $\frac{2}{5}$ $\frac{3}{10}$

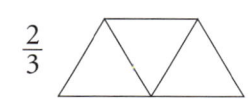

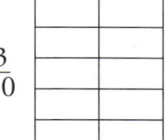

c $\frac{2}{3}$ $\frac{5}{6}$

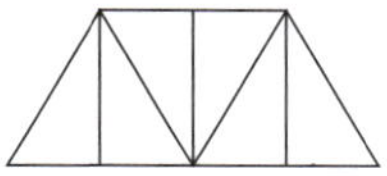

d $\frac{7}{8}$ $\frac{3}{4}$

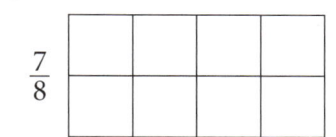

4 Use your calculator to work out which is the larger of the two fractions in each pair.

a $\frac{3}{4}$ and $\frac{7}{10}$ **b** $\frac{6}{20}$ and $\frac{1}{8}$ **c** $\frac{2}{9}$ and $\frac{3}{10}$ **d** $\frac{4}{11}$ and $\frac{6}{19}$

5 Write the symbol < or > between each pair of fractions.

a $\frac{1}{4} \square \frac{3}{8}$ **b** $\frac{4}{5} \square \frac{5}{7}$ **c** $\frac{5}{12} \square \frac{9}{16}$ **d** $\frac{7}{10} \square \frac{17}{25}$

6 Is Sasha correct?
Explain your answer.

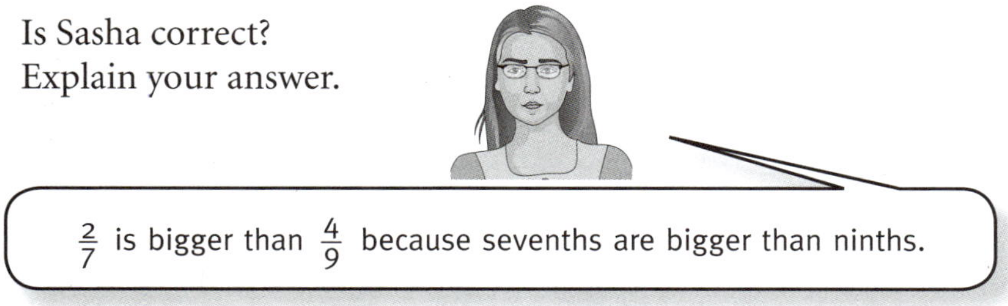

> $\frac{2}{7}$ is bigger than $\frac{4}{9}$ because sevenths are bigger than ninths.

7 What fraction is Ahmad is thinking of?

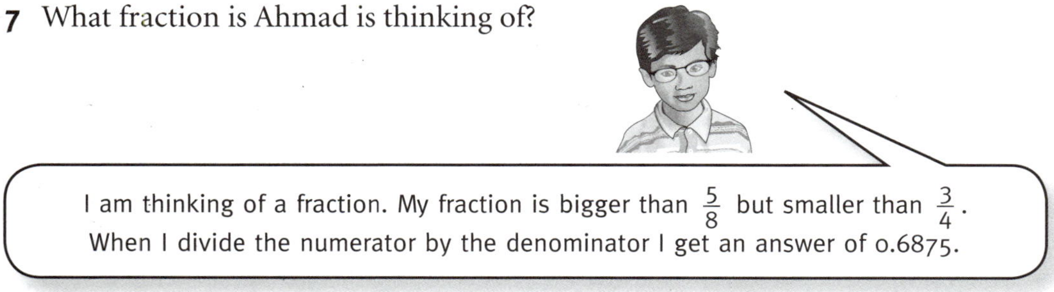

> I am thinking of a fraction. My fraction is bigger than $\frac{5}{8}$ but smaller than $\frac{3}{4}$.
> When I divide the numerator by the denominator I get an answer of 0.6875.

7 Fractions

Exercise 7.4 Improper fractions and mixed numbers

1 For each of these diagrams, write down the fraction shaded as:
  i a mixed number   **ii** an improper fraction.

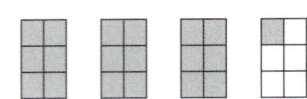

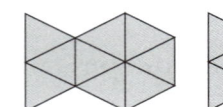

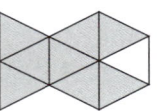

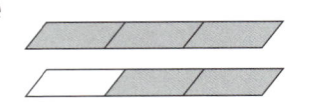

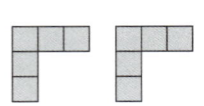

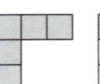

a

b

c

d

e

f

2 Write each improper fraction as a mixed number.

a $\frac{3}{2}$ **b** $\frac{11}{2}$ **c** $\frac{13}{4}$ **d** $\frac{10}{3}$ **e** $\frac{14}{3}$ **f** $\frac{16}{7}$ **g** $\frac{28}{5}$ **h** $\frac{35}{6}$

3 Write each mixed number as an improper fraction.

a $8\frac{1}{2}$ **b** $6\frac{1}{3}$ **c** $2\frac{1}{4}$ **d** $4\frac{1}{7}$ **e** $3\frac{1}{5}$ **f** $2\frac{2}{9}$ **g** $5\frac{4}{5}$ **h** $11\frac{2}{3}$

4 This is part of Alun's homework.
Is Alun correct?
Explain your answer.

Question Change $7\frac{7}{9}$ into a mixed number.

Solution $7 \times 7 = 49$

$49 + 9 = 58$

so $7\frac{7}{9} = \frac{58}{9}$

5 Brad took four boxes of chocolates into work.
There were 12 chocolates in each box.
At the end of the day only five chocolates had <u>not</u> been eaten.
Write the number of boxes of chocolates that <u>were</u> eaten as:
  a a mixed number   **b** an improper fraction.

6 Polly stacked the tins from five boxes of cat food onto an empty shelf in a supermarket.
There were 15 tins of cat food in each box.
At the end of the week there were 20 tins left on the shelf.
The rest of the tins had been sold.
Write the number of boxes of cat food that had been sold, as:
  a a mixed number
  b an improper fraction.
Give your answers in their lowest terms.

7 Fractions

Exercise 7.5 Adding and subtracting fractions

1. Work these out.

   a $\frac{1}{3}+\frac{1}{3}$
   b $\frac{1}{5}+\frac{1}{5}$
   c $\frac{1}{7}+\frac{1}{7}$

   d $\frac{3}{5}+\frac{1}{5}$
   e $\frac{4}{11}+\frac{2}{11}$
   f $\frac{2}{5}-\frac{1}{5}$

   g $\frac{5}{9}-\frac{1}{9}$
   h $\frac{6}{7}-\frac{2}{7}$
   i $\frac{8}{15}-\frac{4}{15}$

2. Work out the answers to these additions and subtractions.
   Write each answer in its simplest form.

   a $\frac{1}{4}+\frac{1}{4}$
   b $\frac{3}{8}+\frac{1}{8}$
   c $\frac{1}{10}+\frac{3}{10}$

   d $\frac{1}{6}+\frac{5}{6}$
   e $\frac{5}{9}-\frac{2}{9}$
   f $\frac{7}{12}-\frac{1}{12}$

   g $\frac{8}{15}-\frac{3}{15}$
   h $\frac{9}{10}-\frac{1}{10}$
   i $\frac{11}{20}-\frac{7}{20}$

3. Work out the answers to these additions.
   Write each answer as a mixed number in its simplest form.

   a $\frac{2}{3}+\frac{2}{3}$
   b $\frac{4}{5}+\frac{3}{5}$
   c $\frac{7}{12}+\frac{7}{12}$

   d $\frac{11}{20}+\frac{17}{20}$
   e $\frac{5}{8}+\frac{7}{8}$
   f $\frac{17}{18}+\frac{5}{18}$

4. Work out the answers to these additions and subtractions.
   Write each answer in its simplest form.

   a $\frac{1}{3}+\frac{1}{6}$
   b $\frac{1}{5}+\frac{3}{10}$
   c $\frac{1}{4}+\frac{3}{8}$

   d $\frac{1}{9}+\frac{2}{3}$
   e $\frac{2}{3}-\frac{1}{6}$
   f $\frac{11}{15}-\frac{2}{5}$

   g $\frac{11}{12}-\frac{3}{4}$
   h $\frac{1}{2}-\frac{5}{22}$
   i $\frac{4}{5}-\frac{3}{10}$

5. Work out the answers to these additions.
   Write each answer in its simplest form and as a mixed number.

   a $\frac{1}{2}+\frac{3}{4}$
   b $\frac{5}{12}+\frac{5}{6}$
   c $\frac{1}{2}+\frac{5}{8}$

   d $\frac{4}{5}+\frac{9}{20}$
   e $\frac{2}{3}+\frac{5}{9}$
   f $\frac{3}{5}+\frac{7}{10}$

6. Zalika adds together two <u>proper</u> fractions.
   The fractions have <u>different</u> denominators.
   She gets an answer of $1\frac{5}{8}$.
   Write down two fractions that Zalika may have added.

   $\square + \square = 1\frac{5}{8}$

7 Fractions

Exercise 7.6 Finding fractions of a quantity

1. Work these out mentally.

   a $\frac{1}{2}$ of $12
   b $\frac{1}{4}$ of 20 cm
   c $\frac{1}{3}$ of 9 kg

   d $\frac{1}{10}$ of 40 mm
   e $\frac{1}{6} \times 12$
   f $\frac{1}{5} \times 30$

2. Work these out mentally.

   a $\frac{2}{5}$ of 10 mm
   b $\frac{3}{4}$ of 40 km
   c $\frac{5}{6}$ of $12

   d $\frac{4}{9}$ of 18 kg
   e $\frac{3}{7} \times 21$
   f $\frac{2}{3} \times 12$

3. Use a written method or a calculator to work these out.

   a $\frac{1}{5}$ of $275
   b $\frac{4}{5}$ of 315 km
   c $\frac{1}{7}$ of 161 m

   d $\frac{3}{7}$ of 224 l
   e $\frac{5}{8} \times 184$
   f $\frac{6}{11} \times 154$

4. A choir has 129 members.
   $\frac{1}{3}$ of the members are male.

   a How many of the choir are male?
   b What fraction of the choir are female?
   c How many of the choir are female?

5. Which of these cards is the odd one out?

   $30 \times \frac{3}{5}$ $32 \times \frac{5}{8}$ $36 \times \frac{5}{9}$

   Explain your answer.

6. At a football match in the Nou Camp Stadium in Barcelona there were 96 455 fans.

   $\frac{3}{5}$ of the fans were supporting Barcelona.

   The rest were supporting Real Madrid.
   How many of the fans were supporting Real Madrid?

7. Alandra takes part in a charity cycle ride from Amsterdam to Brussels.
   The total distance is 208 km.
   After three days she has cycled $\frac{5}{16}$ of the total distance.

   How many kilometres has she still got to cycle?

7 Fractions

Exercise 7.7 Finding remainders

1 Work out these divisions.
Write the remainders as fractions.
  a 9 ÷ 2   **b** 13 ÷ 3   **c** 12 ÷ 5   **d** 9 ÷ 4   **e** 13 ÷ 6   **f** 20 ÷ 9   **g** 27 ÷ 5

2 Work out these divisions.
Write the remainders as fractions in their simplest form.
  a 10 ÷ 4   **b** 26 ÷ 6   **c** 18 ÷ 8   **d** 42 ÷ 10   **e** 27 ÷ 12   **f** 15 ÷ 9   **g** 42 ÷ 4

3 Fenyang uses this method to work out some harder divisions.
Use Fenyang's method to work these out.
  a 257 ÷ 2   **b** 323 ÷ 4
  c 514 ÷ 3   **d** 219 ÷ 6
  e 218 ÷ 4   **f** 526 ÷ 8

Question Work out 274 ÷ 4.

Solution

$$4 \overline{)2\ ^27\ ^34} = 6\ 8 \text{ remainder } 2$$

$274 ÷ 4 = 68\frac{2}{4}$
$= 68\frac{1}{2}$

4 Kagiso uses her calculator to work out some harder divisions.
This is the method she uses.
Use Kagiso's method to work these out.
  a 542 ÷ 15   **b** 848 ÷ 13
  c 582 ÷ 12   **d** 876 ÷ 16
  e 614 ÷ 18   **f** 872 ÷ 24

Question Work out 624 ÷ 14.

Solution 624 ÷ 14 = 44.571...
14 goes into 624 just over 44 times
14 × 44 = 616
624 − 616 = 8 (remainder)
Answer = $44\frac{8}{14}$
   = $44\frac{4}{7}$

5 A group of 340 students travels by bus.
Each bus holds 52 students.
  a How many buses do they need?   **b** How many empty seats will there be?

6 Adelaide has 80 cents to spend on pencils.
Each pencil costs 12 cents.
How many pencils can Adelaide buy?

7 Kaelan has 300 seeds to plant into trays.
Each tray holds 36 seeds.
He plants all the seeds.
How many trays does Kaelan use?

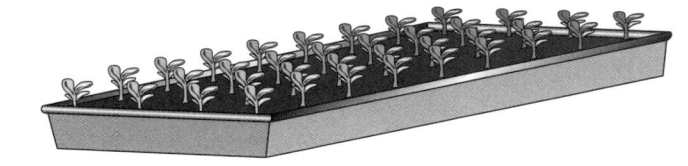

8 A ride at a funfair takes 64 people each time.
There are 280 people waiting to go on the ride.
How many times will the ride have to go before they have all been on the ride?

8 Symmetry

◆ Exercise 8.1 Recognising and describing 2D shapes and solids

1 Write down the name of the 2D shape that is being described each time.
   a I have three sides.
      Two of my angles are the same size and two of my sides are the same length.
   b I have four sides that are not all the same length.
      My opposite sides are the same length.
      My opposite angles are the same size, but I have no right angles.

2 A card has a kite and a circle drawn on it.
   The card is turned three times.

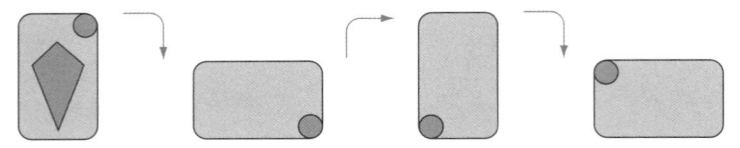

   Copy the cards and draw the missing kite on each of them.

3 Copy this table. Use the words and numbers from the box to complete your table.
   You should not have any spare words or numbers.

   cuboid   square-based pyramid
   triangular-based pyramid
   triangular prism   4 4 5 6 6 6

Name of solid	Number of faces	Number of edges	Number of vertices
	5	8	
	5	9	
		12	8

4 Write down the name of the solid shape that Harsha is describing.

   > I put two identical solid shapes together. The number of faces on the new shape is two more than the number on one of the original shapes.

5 Write down the name of the two shapes that Anders is describing.

   > I have two 2D shapes, with a total of seven sides and seven vertices. I can join them together to form a new shape that has three sides and three vertices.

6 Write down the names of the two solid shapes that Tanesha is describing.

   > I have two solid shapes. I can join them together to form a new shape that has nine faces, 16 edges and nine vertices.

Exercise 8.2 Recognising line symmetry

1 Each of these shapes has either one or two lines of symmetry.

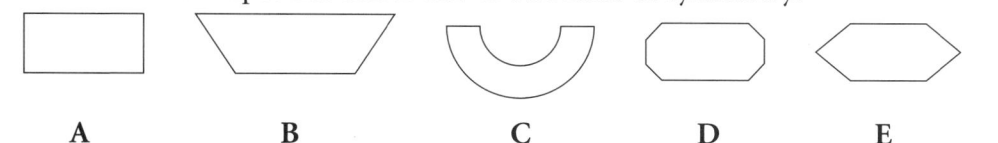

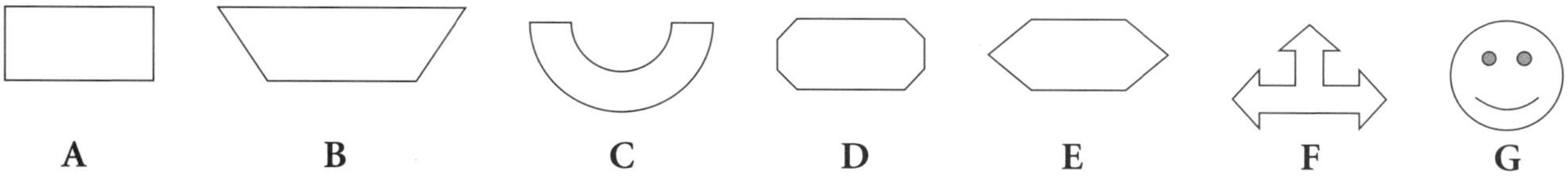

A   B   C   D   E   F   G

Copy and complete the table. Shape **A** has been done for you.

Shape	One line of symmetry	Two lines of symmetry
		A

2 Write down the number of lines of symmetry for each of these shapes.

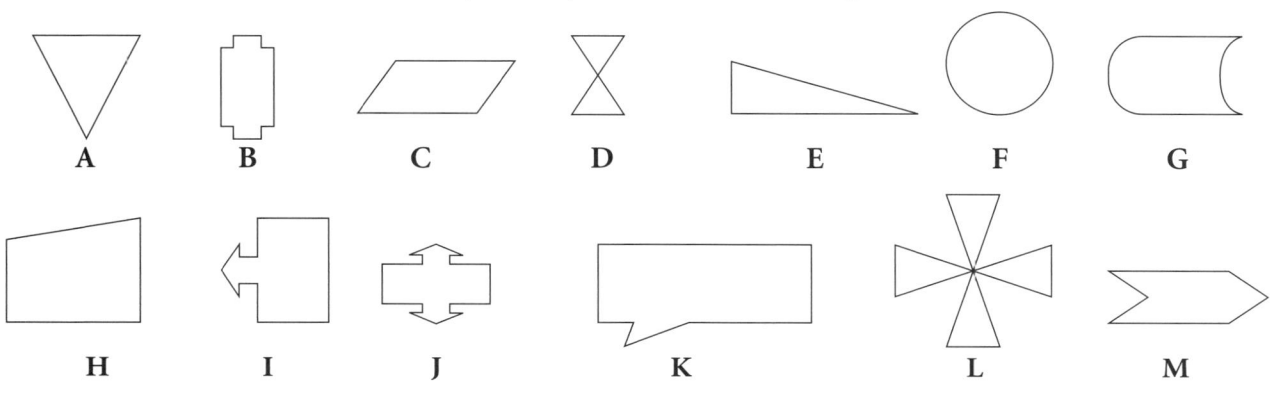

A   B   C   D   E   F   G

H   I   J   K   L   M

3 In each diagram, the thick dotted lines are lines of symmetry. Copy and complete each diagram by shading squares.

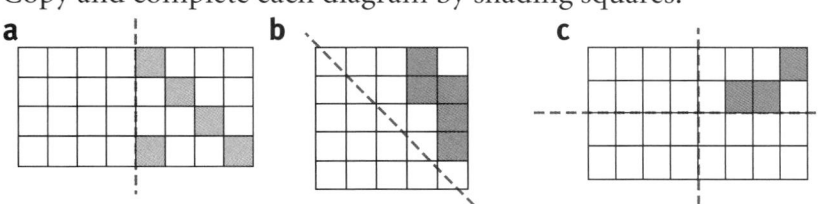

a   b   c

Only shade as many squares as you need to, to make the diagram symmetrical.

4 Copy these patterns onto squared paper.

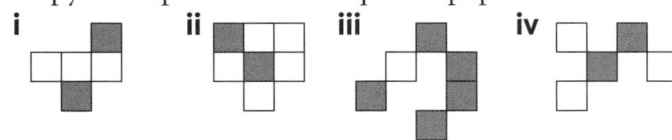

i   ii   iii   iv

  a Look at each pattern and decide how you can change it to give it exactly one line of symmetry.
     You may only add one more grey square.
     You must only make one change for each diagram.
  b Draw the line of symmetry onto each of your patterns.
  c Write down whether your shape has a horizontal, vertical or diagonal line of symmetry.

5 Jacob has a box of tiles.
All the tiles have the same pattern.
The pattern on the tile is like this.
Jacob uses four of the tiles to make a square pattern.
His pattern has four lines of symmetry.
Draw two different patterns that Jacob could make.

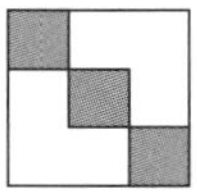

8 Symmetry

Exercise 8.3 Recognising rotational symmetry

1. Write down the order of rotational symmetry of each of these shapes.

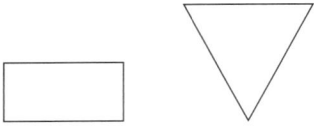

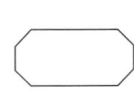

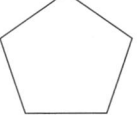

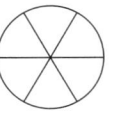

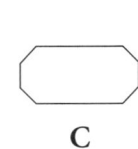

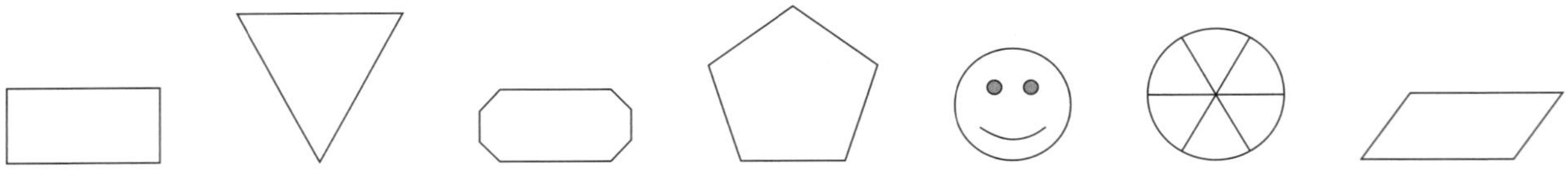

   A   B   C   D   E   F   G

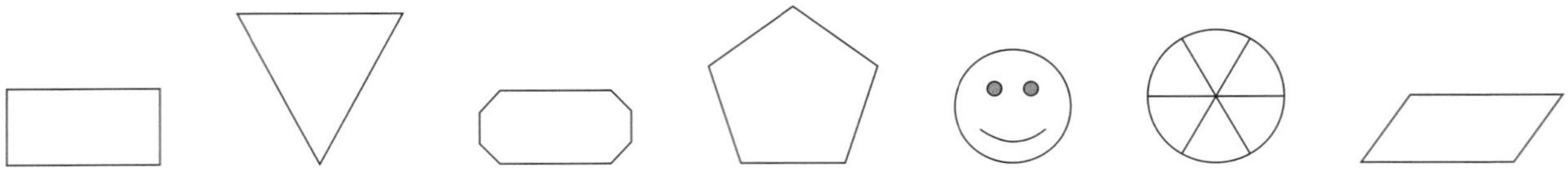

   A   B   C   D   E   F   G

2. Copy this table.
   Write the letter of each shape in the correct space in the table.
   Shape **A** has been done for you.

	Number of lines of symmetry				
Order of rotational symmetry	0	1	2	3	4
1					
2					
3					
4					A

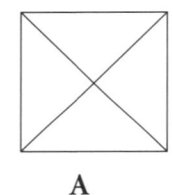

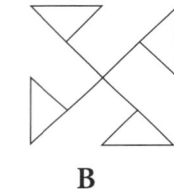

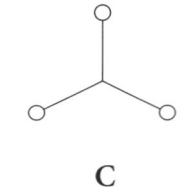

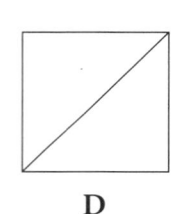

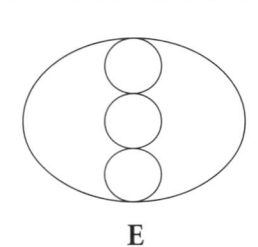

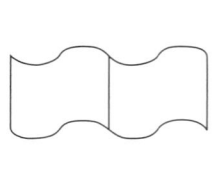

   A   B   C   D   E   F

3. Jason has six white tiles and three grey tiles.
   Each tile is an equilateral triangle.

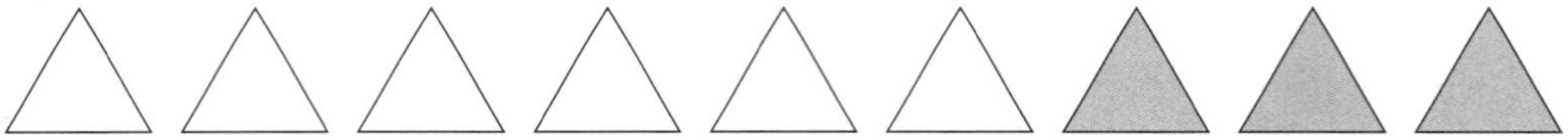

   Jason wants to arrange the tiles to form a pattern with order 3 rotational symmentry
   Draw two patterns to show how he could do this.

4. Toby is making a pattern from grey and white squares.
   This is what he has drawn so far.
   Make four copies of the diagram. 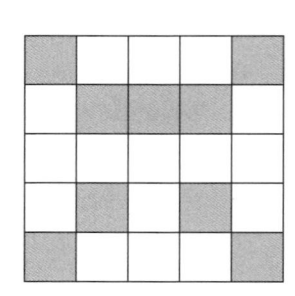
   a Start with three of your copies of the diagram.
      In each one, shade three more squares so that the pattern has rotational symmetry of order 2.
      Each pattern must be different.
   b In your fourth copy of the diagram, shade three more squares so that the pattern has rotational symmetry of order 4.

8 Symmetry

Exercise 8.4 Symmetry properties of triangles, special quadrilaterals and polygons

1 Copy this table.

		Sides			
		all different	1 equal pair	2 equal pairs	all equal
Angles	all different				
	1 equal pair				
	2 equal pairs				
	all equal				A

Write the letter of each shape in the correct space in the table. Shape A has been done for you.
A: square   B: kite   C: rectangle   D: scalene triangle   E: parallelogram
F: isosceles trapezium   G: trapezium   H: equilateral triangle   I: rhombus   J: isosceles triangle

2 Copy this table.

		Rotational symmetry			
		order 1	order 2	order 3	order 4
Number of lines of symmetry	0				
	1				
	2				
	3				
	4				A

Write the letter of each shape in the correct space in the table. Shape A has been done for you.
A: square   B: kite   C: rectangle   D: scalene triangle   E: parallelogram
F: isosceles trapezium   G: trapezium   H: equilateral triangle   I: rhombus   J: isosceles triangle

3 Describe the <u>similarities</u> between an isosceles triangle and an isosceles trapezium.
4 Describe the <u>differences</u> between a square and a rhombus.

5 A, B, C, D, E and F are six points on this grid.
X is another point on the grid.
What are the coordinates of point X when
 a ABCX is a parallelogram?
 b ABDX is a square?
 c ABDX is a kite?
 d ABEX is a rectangle?
 e ABFX is an isosceles trapezium?

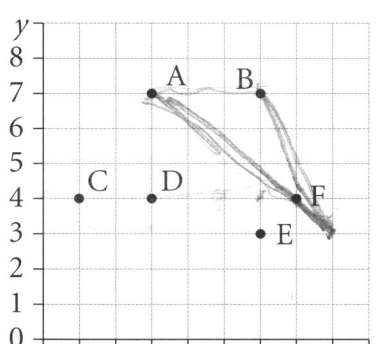

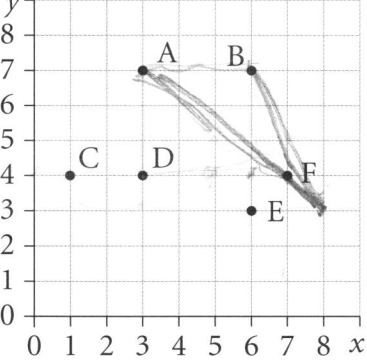

8 Symmetry   49

9 Expressions and equations

Exercise 9.1 Collecting like terms

1. Pita has striped, checked and spotted bricks.
   The length of a striped brick is x.
   The length of a checked brick is y.
   The length of a spotted brick is z.
   Work out the total length of each arrangement of bricks.
   Give each answer in its simplest form.

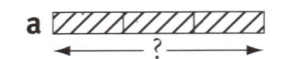

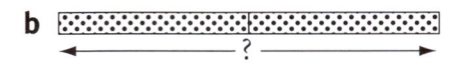

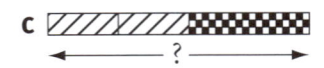

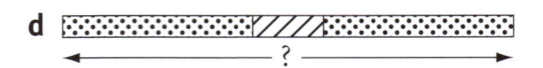

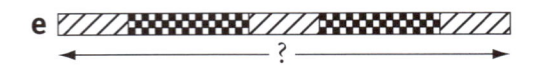

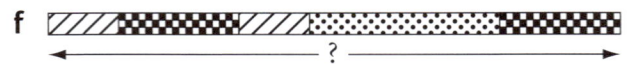

   a, b, c, d, e, f

2. Simplify each expression.
   a $a + a + a + a$
   b $4b + 3b$
   c $4c + 7c$
   d $2d + 3d + 4d$
   e $6e + 6e + e$
   f $10f + f + 4f$
   g $9g - 3g$
   h $4h - 3h$
   i $9i - i$
   j $8j + 2j - 4j$
   k $k + 6k - 3k$
   l $12y - 4y - 7y$

3. In an algebraic pyramid, you find the expression in each block by <u>adding</u> the expressions in the two blocks below it.
   Copy and complete these pyramids.

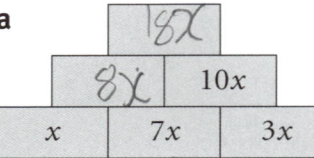

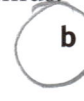

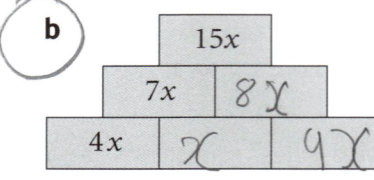

   a: top 18x; middle 8x, 10x; bottom x, 7x, 3x
   b: top 15x; middle 7x, 8x; bottom 4x, x, 9x* [*handwritten answers: 18x, 8x, 8x, x, 9x]

4. Simplify these expressions by collecting like terms.
   a $3x + 4x + 5y$
   b $5z + 5z + 5a + a$
   c $3a + 4b + 4a + 5b$
   d $4x + 5 + 3x + 2$
   e $d + 1 + d + 1$
   f $5f - 3f + 12g - 3g$
   g $45 - 15 + 12w - w$
   h $7x + 5y - 3x + y$
   i $8a + 6b - 4a - 5b$
   j $4w + 3x + 7y - 2w - 3x + 13y$
   k $200a + 20g + 100 - 15g - 70$

5. Write each expression in its simplest form.
   a $4ab + 2ab + 3xy + 5xy$
   b $3rd + 3rd + 5th + 6th$
   c $5tv + 6tv + 9jk - 5kj$
   d $8ej + 7yh - 3je - 4hy$
   e $5v + 15rv - 2v + vr$
   f $7un - 4nu + 11ef - 11fe$

6 This is part of Maddi's homework.

> *Question* Write these expressions in their simplest form.
> a $2x + 8 + 7x - 4$ b $5rg + 4t - t + 2gr$
> *Solution* a $2x + 8 \;\; 10x, 7x - 4 = 3x, 10x + 3x = 13x$
> b $5rg + 4t - t + 2gr = 5rg + 4 + 2gr$

Maddi has made several mistakes.
Explain what Maddi has done wrong.

7 Copy and complete this algebraic pyramid.
Remember, you find the expression in each block by <u>adding</u> the expressions in the two blocks below it.

Pyramid (with student's handwritten answers):
- Top: $17a + 11b$
- Row: $8a + 6b$ | $9a + 5b$ (handwritten)
- Row: $3a + 4b$ (handwritten) | $5a + 2b$ | $4a + 3b$ (handwritten)
- Bottom: $3b$ (handwritten) | $3a + b$ (handwritten) | $2a + b$ | $2a + 2b$ (handwritten)

Exercise 9.2 Expanding brackets

1 Expand the brackets.
   a $3(a + 2)$ b $5(b + 3)$ c $3(c + 2)$ d $5(d - 1)$
   e $4(e - 9)$ f $3(f - 8)$ g $4(2 + f)$ h $8(7 + z)$
   i $9(3 + y)$ j $4(4 - x)$ k $7(1 - w)$ l $7(2 - v)$

2 Multiply out the brackets.
   a $5(2p + 1)$ b $7(3q + 2)$ c $9(2r + 3)$ d $11(3s - 4)$
   e $2(2t - 5)$ f $4(5u - 1)$ g $6(1 + 2v)$ h $8(6 + 4w)$
   i $10(6 + 7x)$ j $5(3 - 5x)$ k $5(4 - 3x)$ l $5(5 - 8x)$

3 This is part of Paul's homework.
Paul has made a mistake on every question.

> *Question* Multiply out the brackets.
> a $5(a + 3)$ b $3(4b - 5)$ c $4(3 - c)$
> *Solution* a $5(a + 3) = 5a + 3$
> b $3(4b - 5) = 12b - 8$
> c $4(3 - c) = 12 - 4c$
> $= 8c$

Explain what Paul has done wrong.

4 Which one of these expressions is the odd one out?
Explain your answer.
$2(9x + 12)$ $2(10x + 8)$ $6(4 + 3x)$ $3(8 + 6x)$ $1(18x + 24)$

9 Expressions and equations   51

Exercise 9.3 Constructing and solving equations

1. Solve each of these equations.
   Check your answers.
   - **a** $x + 2 = 6$
   - **b** $x + 6 = 9$
   - **c** $4 + x = 11$
   - **d** $15 + x = 21$
   - **e** $x - 5 = 10$
   - **f** $x - 4 = 6$
   - **g** $x - 15 = 12$
   - **h** $5x = 20$
   - **i** $3x = 30$
   - **j** $4x = 28$
   - **k** $\frac{x}{5} = 10$
   - **l** $\frac{x}{3} = 9$
   - **m** $\frac{x}{2} = 8$

2. Solve each of these equations and check your answers.
   - **a** $14 = x + 3$
   - **b** $9 = x + 5$
   - **c** $12 = x - 6$
   - **d** $20 = x - 5$
   - **e** $14 = 2x$
   - **f** $50 = 10x$
   - **g** $6 = \frac{x}{3}$
   - **h** $8 = \frac{x}{8}$

3. Solve each of these equations.
   Check your answers.
   - **a** $3x + 2 = 11$
   - **b** $5x + 1 = 11$
   - **c** $4x - 2 = 18$
   - **d** $2x - 8 = 18$
   - **e** $\frac{y}{2} + 5 = 7$
   - **f** $\frac{y}{3} + 3 = 6$
   - **g** $\frac{y}{4} - 5 = 6$
   - **h** $\frac{y}{5} - 2 = 0$
   - **i** $17 = 5z + 2$
   - **j** $18 = 3z - 3$
   - **k** $5 = \frac{z}{4} + 2$
   - **l** $2 = \frac{y}{10} - 6$

4. **a** I think of a number and then add 5. My answer is 21. What is the number I first thought of?

   b I think of a number and then subtract 5. My answer is 21. What is the number I first thought of?

5. Write an equation for each of these and solve it to find the value of the unknown number.
   - **a** I think of a number and multiply it by 5. The answer is 20.
   - **b** I think of a number and divide it by 5. The answer is 20.
   - **c** I think of a number, I multiply it by 5 then add 5. The answer is 20.
   - **d** I think of a number, I divide it by 5 then subtract 5. The answer is 4.

6. In each of these, the total length of each set of bricks is given.
   Write an equation involving the lengths of the bricks, then solve your equation.

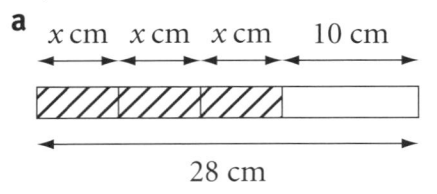

   a x cm, x cm, x cm, 10 cm; total 28 cm

   b y cm, 20 cm, y cm; total 25 cm

10 Averages

Exercise 10.1 Average and range

1. A group of students were timed as they completed a task.

   12 12 14 14 15 18
   20 20 20 29 36

   Their times, in seconds, are listed above.
   Work out: **a** the mode   **b** the median   **c** the range.

2. Maria had 20 pairs of shoes, in the following colours.

   | black black black black black black blue blue blue brown brown green green red red white white white white yellow |

   Find, if you can: **a** the mode   **b** the median   **c** the range.
   If any is impossible to find, explain why.

3. A science class took a test. Here are their marks.

   32 35 35 38 39 41 44 44 44 46

   a Work out: **i** the mode   **ii** the median   **iii** the range.

   The teacher doubles all the marks to change them to percentages.
   b Work out: **i** the new mode   **ii** the new median   **iii** the new range.

4. These are the masses of 10 babies born over a weekend.

   3.1 kg   3.3 kg   3.0 kg   3.3 kg   2.9 kg
   3.0 kg   3.5 kg   3.4 kg   2.6 kg   3.5 kg

   a A nurse writes:

   The range is 3.5 − 3.1 = 0.4 kg.

   i What mistake has the nurse made?   **ii** What is the correct answer?
   b Work out the median mass.

5. There are 20 students in a class.
   The height of the tallest is 1.81 m and of the shortest is 1.52 m.
   A new student joins the class. The range of heights is now 0.32 m.
   How tall is the new student?

6 This table shows how far people who work in an office travel to work.

Distance (km)	less than 5	5 or more but less than 10	10 or more but less than 20	20 or more but less than 30	30 or more
Number of people	9	23	6	9	3

  a How many people travel less than 20 km?
  b What is the modal class?
  c Hassan said: 'More than half the people are in the modal class.' Is this true or false?

7 This table shows how many days some people worked, over a period of two weeks.

Number of days	4	5	6	7	8	9	10
Number of people	4	1	1	4	6	10	2

  a How many people worked less than 7 days?
  b How many people worked more than 7 days?
  c Work out the modal number of days worked.
  d Work out the median number of days worked.

8 Four lengths have a mode of 12 km and a range of 5 km. One of the lengths is 14 km. What are the other three lengths?

Exercise 10.2 The mean

1 Miguel had five oranges.
  Their masses are given in the box.   150 g 170 g 185 g 190 g 190 g
  a Work out the mean mass.
  b Which is greater, the mean or the median?
  c A sixth orange has a mass of 225 g.
    Calculate the mean mass of the six oranges.

2 Andrew recorded the rainfall, in millimetres, each day for two weeks.

First week (mm)	2	0	0	4	3	5	0
Second week (mm)	0	0	0	3	1	1	2

  a Work out the modal rainfall for each week.
  b Work out the mean rainfall for each week.
  c Work out the mean rainfall over the whole two-week period.

3 A community centre has several rooms.
  There are 20 chairs in each of six rooms.
  There are 30 chairs in each of another four rooms.
  Work out the mean number of chairs per room.

4 Sen has been doing jobs to earn money.
  The amounts he has earned for his last six jobs are shown in the box. $25 $15 $20 $85 $10 $25
  a What was the mean amount?
  b Copy and complete this sentence.
    Sen earned less than the mean in ☐ of his jobs.

10 Averages

5 Matches are sold in boxes.
Tomas counted the matches in each of 40 boxes. Here are his results.

Number of matches	47	48	49	50	51	52	53	54
Number of boxes	3	8	12	7	6	2	1	1

   a Work out the range of the number of matches.
   b Calculate the mean number of matches per box.
   c It says on the box: 'Average: 50 matches'. Is this correct?
       Give a reason for your answer.

6 Mia did a survey.
She stood at the school gate and counted the number of people in each car that passed her.

Number of people	1	2	3	4	5	6
Number of cars	15	9	4	2	1	1

   a How many cars passed Mia?
   b Work out the mean number of people per car.

7 The mean age of nine members of a club is 20 years.
When another person joins the club, the mean age increases to 21 years.
How old is the new person?

Exercise 10.3 Comparing distributions

1 Here are the ages, in years, of the cars in two car parks.

Car park A: 4   8   9   7   2   10   7
Car park B: 1   4   3   5   6   4   1   4   3

   a Work out the median age for each car park.
   b Work out the range of ages for each car park.
   c Which car park has the older cars, on average?
   d Which car has greater variation in ages?

2 Sami made 27 phone calls in 12 days.
Marta made 45 phone calls in 18 days.
   a Work out the mean number of calls
       per day for each person.
   b Who made more calls per day?

3 Here are two sets of test marks. Both are marked out of 50.

Test 1:   32   35   39   26   21   34   20   25   19   36
Test 2:   27   33   14   38   39   35   44   16   35   18   41   37   31   29   35

   a Work out the median for each test.
   b Use the medians to decide which test was harder.
   c Which test shows a greater variation in marks?

4 Raj and Tamasa both drive to work.
They record the times their journeys take for a number of days.
Here are their results, The times are in minutes.

| Raj: | 23 | 31 | 29 | 40 | 27 | 30 | 37 | | | |
| Tamasa: | 28 | 26 | 22 | 30 | 29 | 25 | 28 | 31 | 29 | 22 |

a Work out the mean journey times.
b Work out the range of the times for each person.
c State two facts about Raj's journey times, compared to Tamasa's.

5 Here are some details about two football teams.

Team	Matches played	Matches won	Highest score	Goals scored	Goals against
United	30	20	7 goals	81	42
City	24	16	6 goals	78	36

a Which team scored a higher mean number of goals per match?
b Which team had a higher mean number of goals per match scored against them?

6 The half-marathon times for two runners are given below.
They are given to the nearest minute.

| Jaouad: | 63 | 65 | 63 | 62 | 64 | 67 | 64 | 64 | | |
| Tsegaye: | 61 | 64 | 66 | 63 | 65 | 66 | 70 | 60 | 62 | 64 |

a Compare the average speeds of the two runners.
Work out any numbers you need to help you do this.
b Compare the variations between the times for each runner.
Which runner is more consistent?

7 Some students were asked to estimate the length and the mass of a piece of wood.
Their results are shown in this table.

	Number	Mean estimated length (cm)	Range of estimated lengths (cm)	Mean estimated mass (g)	Range of estimated masses (g)
Boys	37	16.5	5.2	285	70
Girls	28	17.8	4.1	194	95

Say whether these statements are TRUE, FALSE or if you CANNOT TELL.
a There is more variation in the boys' estimates of the length than in the girls' estimates.
b On average, the boys' estimates of the length were greater than the girls' estimates.
c The boys' estimates of the length were better than the girls' estimates.
d On average, the girls' estimates of the mass were smaller than the boys' estimates.
e The girls' estimates of the mass were better than the boys' estimates.

11 Percentages

Exercise 11.1 Simple percentages

1. Draw a rectangle. Shade 35% of it.

   > Draw a 10 cm by 1 cm rectangle; it will have an area of 10 cm². Next, work out 35% of 10 cm² and shade that amount in.

2. **a** Estimate what percentage of this strip is shaded.

   b What fraction is not shaded?

3. Write these fractions as percentages.

   a $\frac{9}{10}$ **b** $\frac{9}{20}$ **c** $\frac{9}{25}$ **d** $\frac{9}{50}$

4. $\frac{2}{5}$ $\frac{8}{25}$ $\frac{1}{3}$ $\frac{7}{20}$

   Write these fractions as percentages.
   Use your answers to write the fractions in order, smallest first.

5. $\frac{1}{8} = 12\frac{1}{2}\%$

   Use this fact to write to write $\frac{3}{8}$ as a percentage.

6. Tara and Mina are doing a 20-kilometre walk.
   Tara has completed 8 km and Mina has completed 11 km.
   a What fraction of the walk has each of them completed?
   b What percentage of the walk has each of them completed?

7. By writing these fractions as percentages, show that they add up to 1.

   $\frac{3}{5}$ $\frac{1}{4}$ $\frac{3}{20}$

8. There are 200 passengers on a plane.
   84 of them are women and 12 are children.
   What percentage of them are:
   a women **b** children **c** neither women nor children?

9. 82 people work in Lara's office.
   Last year, 62 people of them went on holiday.
   Which of these percentages is closest to the number that went on holiday?
   45% 55% 65% 75% 85% 95%

10. What is 50 g as a percentage of one kilogram?

Exercise 11.2 Calculating percentages

1 Find 40% of each amount.
  a $50   b 20 kg   c 200 m   d 35 people   e 85 years

2 Copy this table and fill in the missing numbers.

10%	30%	50%	70%	100%
	75			

3 Calculate the following amounts.
  a 80% of 45   b 15% of 90   c $33\frac{1}{3}$% of 75 people   d 27% of 2000 g

4 There are 40 boys and 20 girls at a party.
  35% of the boys and 60% of the girls are wearing sunglasses.
  How many people are wearing sunglasses altogether?

5 Jess wants to save $150.
  So far she has saved 62%.
  How much more does she need?

6 This is part of Anish's answer to a homework question.

> 40% of $70 = $28
> We can halve all the numbers.
> So 20% of $35 = $14.

Is Anish correct?
Give a reason for your answer.

7 60% of a number is 36.
  What is 50% of the same number?

8 Copy these statements and fill in the missing numbers.
  a 50% of 30 cm = $\frac{1}{4}$ of ☐ cm
  b 75% of 36 people = 25% of ☐ people
  c 30% of 80 g = ☐ % of 50 g

11 Percentages

Exercise 11.3 Comparing quantities

1. In class A there are 20 students. 14 of them are girls.
   In class B there are 25 students. 15 of them are girls.
   a Find the percentage of girls in each class.
   b Which class has more girls?
   c Which class has a greater percentage of girls?

2. Hassan scored these marks in three different tests.

	Test 1	Test 2	Test 3
Mark	17	45	63
Total	20	50	75

   a In which test did he score the highest percentage?
   b In which test did he score the lowest percentage?

3. On Thursday, 40 trains left a station. Eight left late.
   On Saturday 50 trains left the station. Nine left late.
   a What percentage of the trains were not late on each day?
   b Which day had the better record for trains being on time?

4. Last year a football team scored at least one goal in 65% of their matches.
   This year they played 40 matches and scored at least one goal in 28 of them.
   Has their performance got better or worse?
   Give a reason for your answer.

5. Last year a political party won 65% of the votes in an election.
   This year the party won 70% of the votes in an election.

   The party got more votes this year.

   Explain why Razi might not be correct.

6. The table shows the populations of two towns.
   The numbers are in thousands.

Town	Aged under 18 (thousands)	Aged over 18 (thousands)
Arcot	14	36
Badam	6	14

   Which town has a greater percentage of people aged under 18?
   Give figures to justify your answer.

11 Percentages

12 Constructions

Exercise 12.1 Measuring and drawing lines

1 Measure the length of each of these lines.
   Give the measurements correct to the nearest mm.
   Write each measurement in: **i** centimetres (cm)   **ii** millimetres (mm).

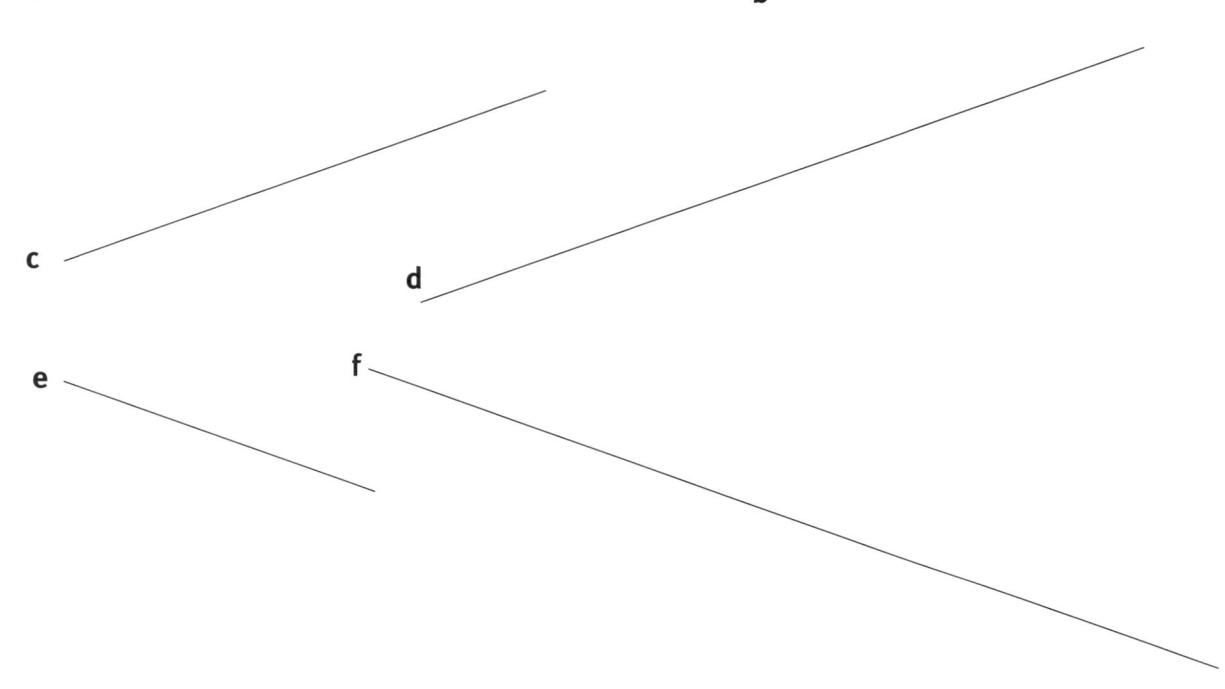

   a ─────────────────────────   b ────

   c, d, e, f (lines shown)

2 Draw straight lines with lengths of:
   a 4 cm   **b** 9.5 cm   **c** 0.8 cm   **d** 12.9 cm.
   Write the length of each line next to it.

Exercise 12.2 Drawing perpendicular and parallel lines

1 Draw two parallel lines that are:
   a 10 cm long and 2 cm apart
   b 6.2 cm long and 4.5 cm apart.

2 Draw the line AB 12 cm long.
   Mark the point C on the line AB, so that C is 4 cm from A.
   Draw a line from C that is perpendicular to the line AB.

3 Draw the line WX 10 cm long.
   Mark the point Y on the line WX so that Y is 3 cm from W.
   Mark the point Z on the line WX so that Z is 4.5 cm from X.
   Draw two lines, one from Y and one from Z, that are both perpendicular to the line WX.

Exercise 12.3 Constructing triangles

1 Draw each of these triangles accurately.

a 6 cm, 60°, 8 cm

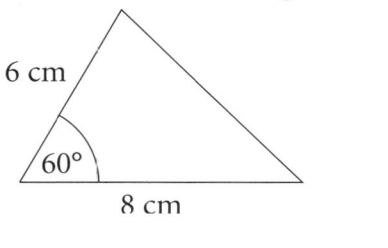

b 6 cm, 35°, 7.5 cm

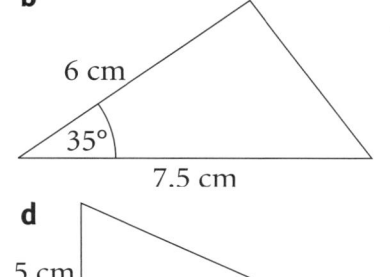

c 10 cm, 20°, 6.5 cm

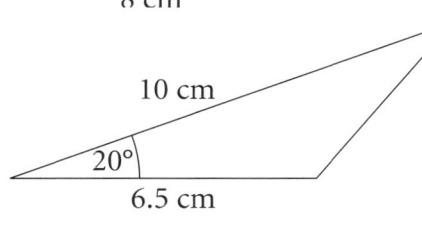

d 5 cm, right angle, 10 cm

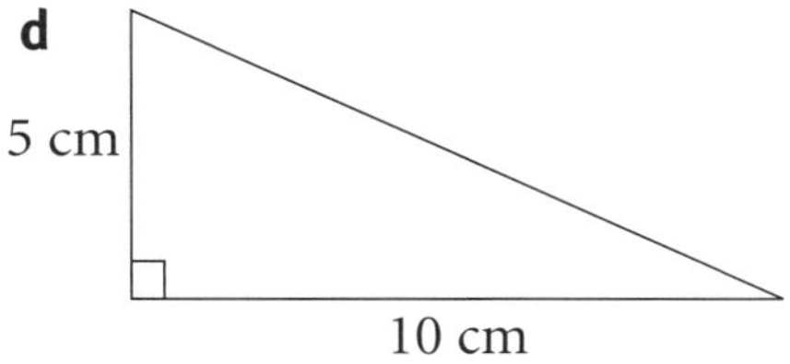

Not drawn accurately

2 Draw each of these triangles accurately.

a 35°, 55°, 8 cm

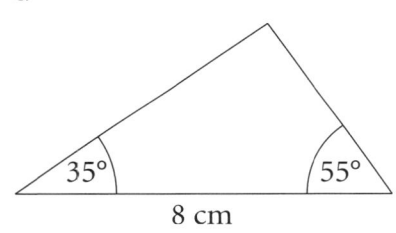

b 40°, 65°, 9.5 cm

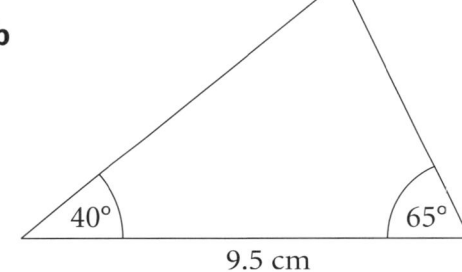

c 50°, 50°, 6.6 cm

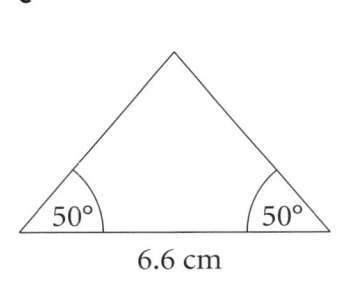

d 40°, right angle, 7 cm

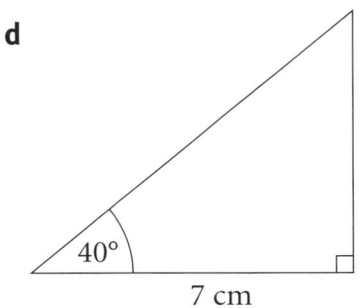

Not drawn accurately

3 a Make an accurate drawing of triangle ABC.
 b Measure and write down the length of side AC.
 c Measure and write down the size of angle BCA.

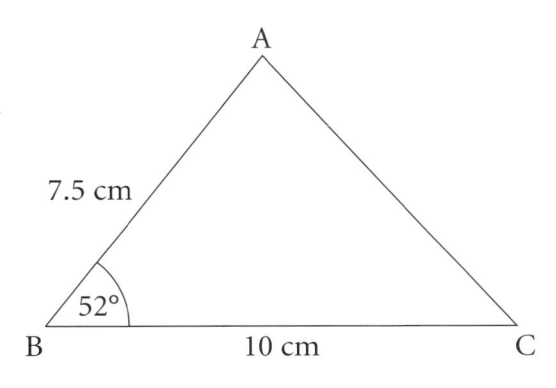

AB = 7.5 cm, angle B = 52°, BC = 10 cm

Not drawn accurately

12 Constructions **61**

4
  a Make an accurate drawing of triangle ABC.
  b Measure and write down the length of side AB.
  c Measure and write down the length of side AC.
  d Measure and write down the size of angle BAC.
  e Work out the total of the three angles in the triangle.
  f Have you have drawn your triangle accurately?
     Give a reason for your answer.

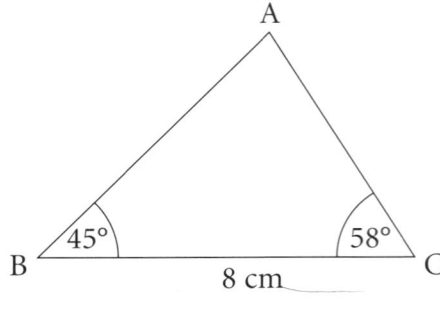

B 45°, C 58°, BC = 8 cm

Not drawn accurately

5 Draw each of these triangles accurately.

a 6 cm, 125°, 6.6 cm

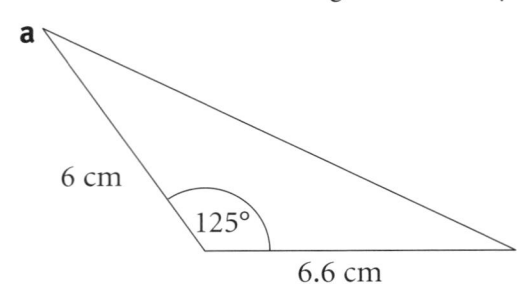

b 10°, 160°, 5 cm

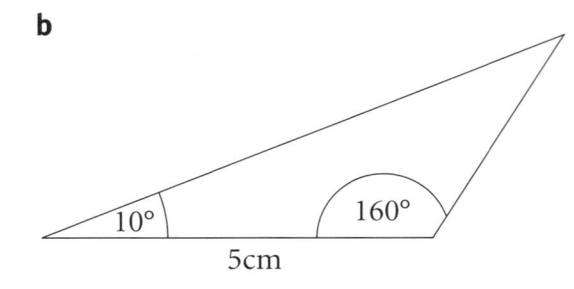

Not drawn accurately

6 Shen and Ahmad have both drawn a triangle ABC.
They are talking about their triangles.

Shen's drawing: B 45°, C 78°, BC = 8 cm

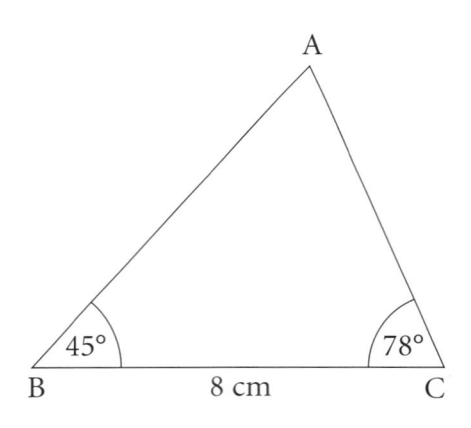

Ahmad's drawing: B 58°, AB = 7 cm, BC = 7 cm

The side AC in my triangle is longer than the side AC in your triangle.

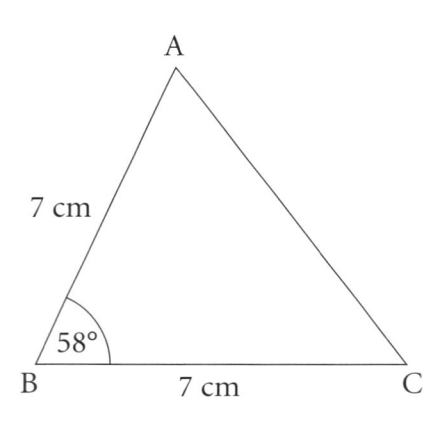

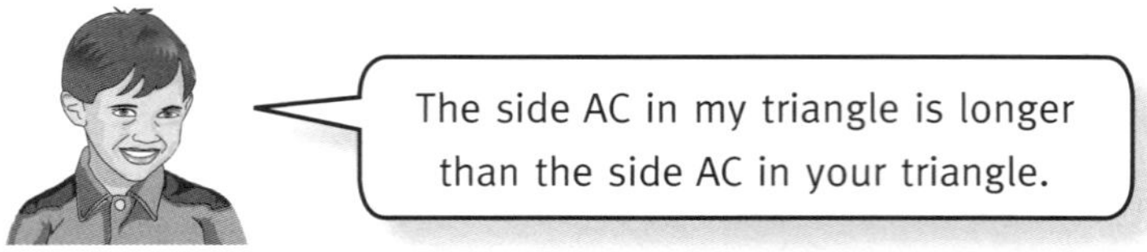

Is what Shen is saying to Ahmad correct?
Show how you worked out your answer.

12 Constructions

Exercise 12.4 Constructing squares, rectangles and polygons

1. Make an accurate drawing of a square with a side length of 6.5 cm.

2. Make an accurate drawing of a rectangle with a length of 8 cm and width 4 cm.

3. Make an accurate drawing of a regular hexagon with a side length of 5 cm and an internal angle of 120°.

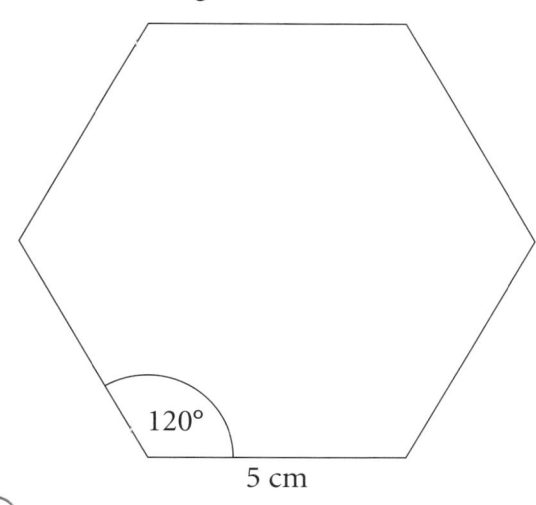

4. Make an accurate drawing of a regular pentagon with a side length of 5 cm and an internal angle of 108°.

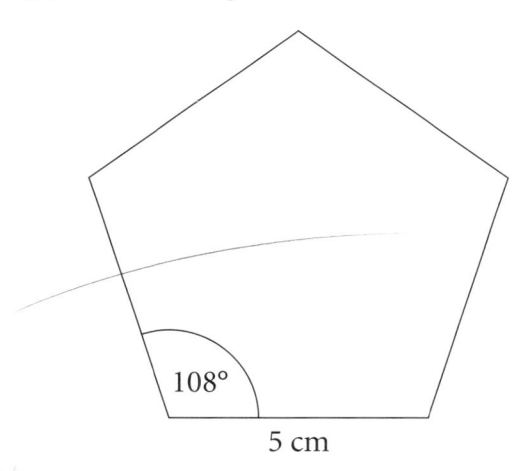

5. The diagram shows two identical rectangles and a square.
   The length of each of the rectangles is four times the length of the side of the square.
   The width of each of the rectangles is equal to the length of the side of the square.
   The square has a side length of 3 cm.
   Make an accurate drawing of the diagram.

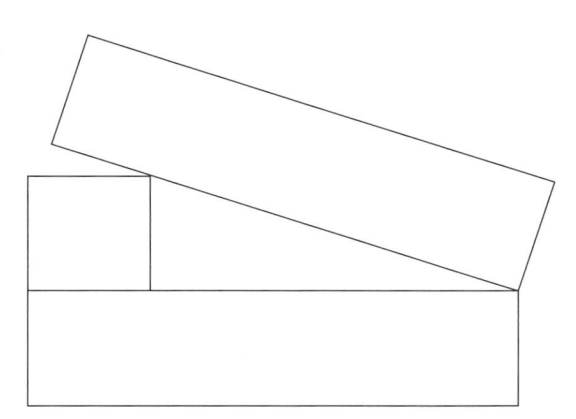

12 Constructions

13 Graphs

Exercise 13.1 Plotting coordinates

1 Write down the coordinates of the points D, E, F and G.

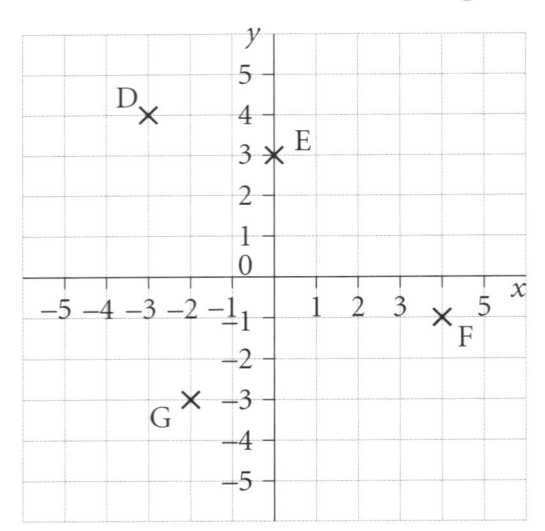

2 **a** Write down the coordinates of P and Q.
  b M is the mid-point of PQ.
     Work out the coordinates of M.

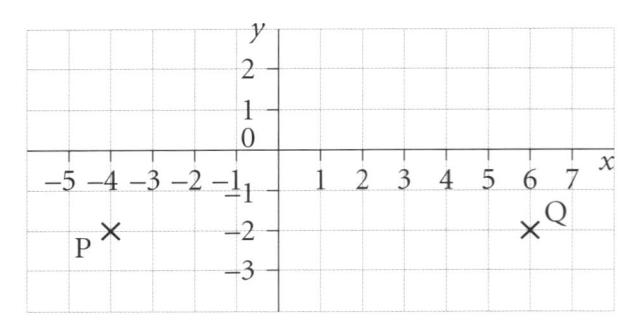

3 **a** Draw a coordinate grid and mark the points R(3, −2) and S(−3, 4).
  b T is the mid-point of RS.
     Work out the coordinates of T.

4 **a** Draw a coordinate grid and mark these points.
     A(5, 2)   B(−3, −2)   C(1, 0)   D(−2, 4)   E(−5, −3)
  b Four of the points are in a straight line. Which is the odd one out?

5 **a** The points (−3, 2), (1, 2) and (1, −2) are three corners of a square.
     Work out the coordinates of the fourth corner of the square.
  b Find the coordinates of the centre of the square.

   The centre of the square is the point where the diagonals meet.

6 The points A(−3, 6), B(2, 1) and C(−3, 1) are the corners of a triangle.
  a Draw the triangle on a coordinate grid.
  b Explain why the triangle is isosceles.

64 13 Graphs

7 Write down the coordinates of:
   a point F
   b the mid-point of AH
   c the mid-point of AB
   d the centre of the octagon

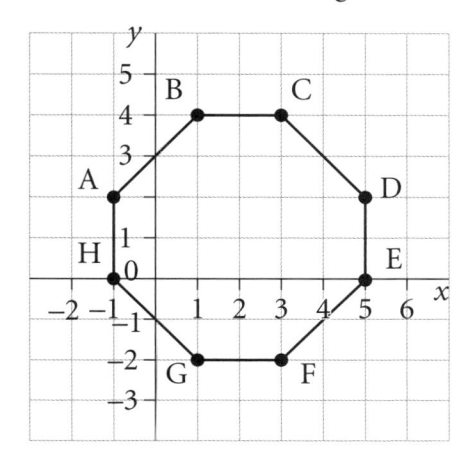

8 a Draw the points A(−6, −5) and M(−2, −1) on a coordinate grid.
   b B is a third point on the same grid.
   M is the mid-point of AB.
   Work out the coordinates of B.

Exercise 13.2 Lines parallel to the axes

1. Work out the equation of the line through each pair of points.
   a A and B
   b B and C
   c C and D
   d D and E

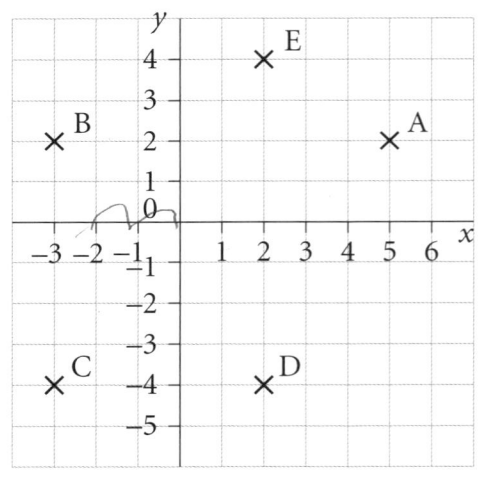

2. Which lettered points on the grid are on these lines?
   a $x = -3$
   b $y = 3$

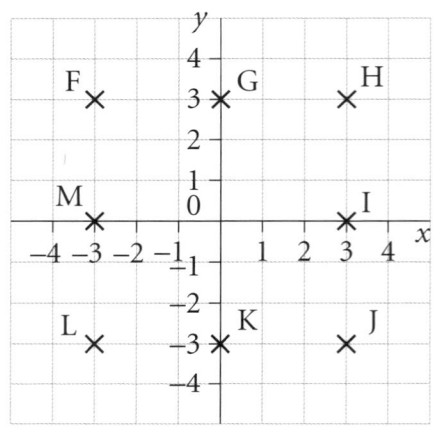

3. Work out the equations of two lines that pass through each point.
   a $(4, 7)$
   b $(-3, -6)$
   c $(0, 9)$

4. a Draw a coordinate grid.
      Draw on your grid the lines with equations $y = 2$, $x = -4$ and $y = -5$.
   b There are two points where lines cross.
      Write down the coordinates of these points.

5. Find the equation of the line through each pair of points.
   a $(4, -5)$ and $(2, -5)$
   b $(3, 3)$ and $(3, -3)$
   c $(2, 0)$ and $(-2, 0)$

6. a Draw a coordinate grid.
      Draw on your grid the lines with equations $x = -2$, $x = -6$, $y = 3$ and $y = 5$.
   b The lines form a rectangle.
      Write down the coordinates of the corners.
   c The rectangle has two lines of symmetry.
      Write down their equations.

7. Three of these points are in a straight line.
   $(3, 6)$ $(-3, -6)$ $(3, -6)$ $(-3, 6)$ $(6, -6)$ $(6, 3)$
   Work out the equation of the line through the three points.

13 Graphs

Exercise 13.3 Other straight lines

1 a Copy and complete this table of values for $y = x + 2$.
  b Draw the graph of $y = x + 2$.

x	−4	−2	0	1	2	4
y	−2				4	

2 a Complete this table of values for $y = 2x$.
  b Draw the graph of $y = 2x$.

x	−2	−1	0	2	3	4
y	−4			4		

3 a Complete this table of values for $y = 2(x + 2)$.
  b Draw the graph of $y = 2(x + 2)$.
  c Where does the graph cross the x-axis?
  d Where does the graph cross the y-axis?

x	−3	−2	0	1	2	3
y			4			10

4 a Complete this table of values for $y = 6 − x$.
  b Draw the graph of $y = 6 − x$.
  c Where does the graph cross the x-axis?

x	−3	−1	0	2	4	5
y			6		2	

5 a Complete this table of values for $y = 7 − 2x$.
  b Draw the graph of $y = 7 − 2x$.

x	−2	0	1	3	5
y		7	5		

6 a Complete this table of values for $y = 2x + 3$.
  b Draw the graph of $y = 2x + 3$.

x	−2	−1	0	2	4
y					

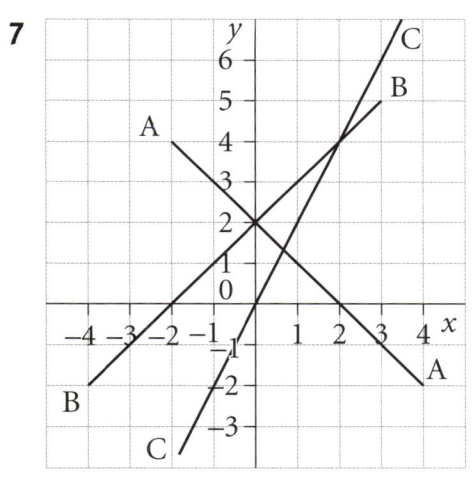

7 This graph shows three lines. They are labelled A, B and C.
The equations of the lines are $y = 2x$, $y = 2 + x$ and $y = 2 − x$.
Match the equations to the lines.

8 a Draw the graph of $y = x + 4$.
  b On the same graph draw the line $y = 2$.
  c Where do the lines cross?

Start with a table of values.

14 Ratio and proportion

◆ Exercise 14.1 Simplifying ratios

1 For each of these necklaces, write down the ratio of black beads to white beads.
   a   b   c   d

2 For each of these necklaces, write down the ratio of white beads to black beads. Give each ratio in its simplest form.
   a   b   c   d

3 For each of these patterns, write down the ratio of grey squares to white squares. Give each ratio in its simplest form.
   a   b

4 Write each of these ratios in its simplest form.
   a 2 : 4   **b** 2 : 20   **c** 3 : 9   **d** 3 : 21   **e** 4 : 16   **f** 4 : 20
   g 24 : 4   **h** 60 : 10   **i** 60 : 3   **j** 21 : 7   **k** 40 : 8   **l** 64 : 8

5 Write each of these ratios in its simplest form.
   a 4 : 18   **b** 4 : 30   **c** 16 : 18   **d** 6 : 15   **e** 8 : 18   **f** 8 : 30
   g 15 : 12   **h** 32 : 12   **i** 55 : 10   **j** 16 : 10   **k** 24 : 15   **l** 21 : 6

6 Jake sees this recipe for Irish soda bread.

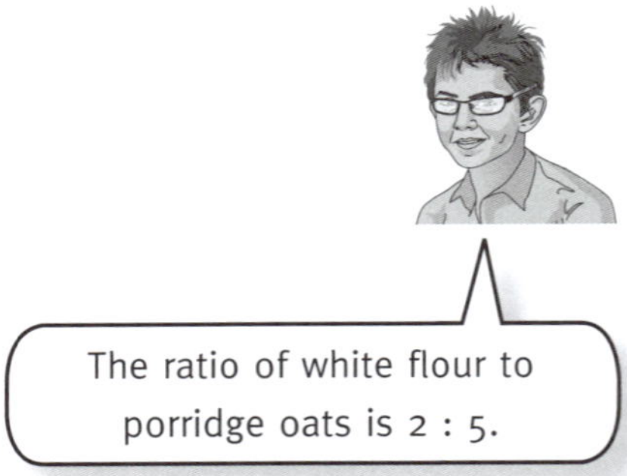

Irish soda bread	
250 g white flour	1 tsp salt
250 g wholemeal flour	1 tsp soda
100 g porridge oats	25 g butter
500 ml buttermilk	

The ratio of white flour to porridge oats is 2 : 5.

Is Jake correct?
Explain your answer.

Exercise 14.2 Sharing in a ratio

1 Copy and complete these workings to share $40 between Ain and Geb in the ratio 1 : 3.

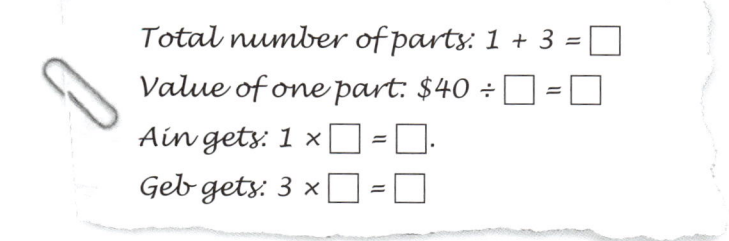

> Total number of parts: 1 + 3 = ☐
> Value of one part: $40 ÷ ☐ = ☐
> Ain gets: 1 × ☐ = ☐.
> Geb gets: 3 × ☐ = ☐

2 Share these amounts between Migina and Tadi in the ratios given.
   a $24 in the ratio 1 : 3
   b $45 in the ratio 1 : 4
   c $49 in the ratio 1 : 6
   d $32 in the ratio 3 : 1
   e $36 in the ratio 5 : 1
   f $32 in the ratio 7 : 1

3 Share these amounts between Yakecan and Nantan in the ratios given.
   a $55 in the ratio 2 : 3
   b $49 in the ratio 3 : 4
   c $64 in the ratio 3 : 5
   d $28 in the ratio 5 : 2
   e $48 in the ratio 7 : 5
   f $28 in the ratio 11 : 3

4 A box of chocolates contains milk chocolates and dark chocolates in the ratio 4 : 3. The box contains 35 chocolates.
How many milk chocolates are there in the box?

5 A factory makes orange paint by mixing red paint and yellow paint in the ratio 7 : 2. The factory makes 2700 litres of orange paint every day.
How many litres of yellow paint does the factory use every day?

6 Cruz and Gloria bought an appartment for $36 000.
Cruz paid $12 000 and Gloria paid the rest.
   a Write the ratio of the amount they each paid in its simplest form.
Two years later they sold the appartment for $42 000.
   b How much money should Gloria get?

7 There are two types of fish in a lake. These are carp and pike.
In a netted area of the lake 120 carp and 16 pike were caught.
In the whole lake it is estimated there are 34 000 fish.

> I estimate that there are 4000 pike in the lake altogether.

Show how Zalika worked out this estimate.

8 Estela and Luiza are going to share 35 dolls, either in the ratio of their ages, or in the ratio of the number of dolls they already have.
Estela is 9 years old and has 24 dolls already.
Luiza is 12 years old and has 36 dolls already.
Which ratio would be better for Estela?
Explain your answer.

Exercise 14.3 Using direct proportion

1 Tiago buys one chicken for $1.20. Work out the cost of:
   a 2 chickens   **b** 10 chickens.

2 Daniel does 2 hours of guitar practice every day. Work out how many hours of practice he does in:
   a 4 days   **b** a week.

3 Luiza goes to the gym 3 times a week.
   Work out how many times she goes to the gym in:
   a 3 weeks   **b** 1 year.

> Remember that there are 52 weeks in a year.

4 Four chorizos weigh 500 grams.
   Copy and complete the workings to find the weight of 7 chorizos.

> 1 chorizo weighs: 500 ÷ 4 = ☐
> 7 chorizos weigh: 7 × ☐ = ☐

5 Five pieces of bacalhau weigh 900 grams.
   Work out the weight of:
   a 1 piece of bacalhau   **b** 7 pieces of bacalhau.

> Bacalhau is salted cod.

6 Joaquim is paid $56 for 8 hours' work.
   How much does she earn when she works for:
   a 4 hours   **b** 12 hours?

7 A *bureau de change* charges €166 for £100.
   How much do they charge for:
   a £50   **b** £250?

8 This is part of Eduardo's homework.

> *Question* A recipe for 4 people uses 280 g of potatoes.
> How much potato does the recipe need for 10 people?
>
> *Solution* The recipe is for 4 people, 4 + 6 = 10
> 4 people need 280 g of potatoes
> 2 people need 280 g ÷ 2 = 140 g potatoes
> 4 + 2 = 6, so 280 + 140 = 420 g
> Altogether the recipe needs 420 g of potato.

Explain what he has done wrong and work out the right answer.

9 A carpenter orders 40 identical pieces of wood.
   The total value of the order is $300.
   He made a mistake in his measuring, so he had to order 10 extra pieces of wood.
   What is the total value of the order now?

14 Ratio and proportion

15 Time

◆ Exercise 15.1 The 12-hour and 24-hour clock

1 Write these 24-hour clock times as 12-hour clock times.
   a 01 20   b 15 45   c 20 20   d 12 35

2 Write these 12-hour clock times as 24-hour clock times.
   a 12 05 am   b 12 34 pm   c 10 50 pm   d 9 20 am

3 How long is it from:
   a 14 15 to 15 25   b 15 28 to 18 52   c 08 40 to 11 24?

4 How long is it from:
   a 12 15 pm to 2 22 pm   b 9 35 am to 1 45 pm   c 6 23 pm to 9 41 pm?

5 a Paul's car journey started at 14 35 and finished at 19 17.
     How long did the journey take Paul?
   b Paul stopped for a rest for $1\frac{1}{4}$ hours during the journey.
     How much time did Paul spend driving?

6 Ali agrees to meet a friend at a restaurant at 1 15 pm.
  It will take Ali 25 minutes to reach the restaurant.
  Ali wants to arrive 10 minutes early.
  What time must Ali set off for the restaurant?

7 a Zac went to see a film that started at 17 44 and finished at 19 31.
     How long was the film?
   b Another film started at 19 23 and lasted 131 minutes.
     What time did it finish?
   c A third film finished at 16 17. It was 93 minutes long.
     What time did it start?

8 Shen caught a train that left the station at 08 42.
  After 46 minutes it arrived at the next station, where it waited for 7 minutes.
  The rest of the journey took 33 minutes.
   a How long did it take Shen for the whole journey?
   b What time did the train arrive at its final destination?

9 The time in New York is 6 hours behind the time in Amsterdam.
   a What is the time in New York when it is 19 15 in Amsterdam?
   b What is the time in Amsterdam when it is 19 15 in New York?

10 A flight from London to Auckland takes 26 hours and 30 minutes.
   The plane leaves London at 15 45 on 5 December.
    a What is the time and date in London when the plane arrives in Auckland?
    b Auckland is 13 hours ahead of London in December.
       What is the time and date in Auckland when the plane arrives?

Exercise 15.2 Timetables

1 Stefan makes a timetable for a visit for a job interview.

Arrival	11 15
Start of tour	11 35
Lunch	12 20
Interview	14 05
End of visit	15 35

  a Write the time for lunch in the 12-hour clock.
  b How long is it between:
   i his arrival and the start of the tour
   ii the start of the tour and the interview
   iii the arrival and the end of his visit?

2 A bus leaves the airport at 13 15.
  20 minutes later it arrives at the hotel.
  12 minutes after that it reaches the zoo.
  17 minutes after that it is in the town centre.
  Write out a timetable for the bus.

3 This is part of a train timetable.

Allerby	11 35	13 10	14 05	15 45
Ditton	11 52	–	14 22	–
Alford	12 18	–	14 48	16 21
Newlin	12 31	–	15 01	–
Catrigg	12 49	14 02	15 19	16 48

  a A boy arrives at Ditton station at 13 50.
   How long must he wait for a train to Newlin?
  b A woman gets on the 11 35 at Allerby.
   How long will it take her to get to Catrigg?
  c Two trains stop at Newlin.
   What is the time interval between them?
  d Ayesha wants to get to Catrigg by 15 00.
   What time should she catch a train from Allerby?

15 Time

4 Here is a bus timetable.

Railway station	08 20	08 35	08 50	09 05	09 20
Bus station	08 47	09 02	09 17	09 32	09 47
Airport	09 12	09 27	09 42	09 57	10 12

Copy and complete these sentences.
- **a** Buses leave the bus station every ____ minutes.
- **b** The journey from the railway station to the airport takes ____ minutes.
- **c** The journey from the bus station to the airport takes ____ minutes.
- **d** To be at the airport at 09 35, catch the bus at the railway station at ____.

5 These are some departure times at a railway station.

Destination	Departure time
Margate	14 42
Bedford	14 48
Brighton	14 53
Sheffield	15 00
Paris	15 08
Dover	15 21
Bedford	15 34

- **a** There are two trains to Bedford.
  What is the time difference between their departure times?
- **b** The time now is 12 42.
  How long is it before the Paris departure?
- **c** The Brighton train is delayed by 35 minutes.
  What is the new departure time?
- **d** The Margate train is due to arrive at its destination at 17 10.
  How long does the journey take?

6 These are the times of buses between two towns.

Alperton	10 45	11 30	12 15
Parcley	11 50	12 35	13 20

Parcley	13 10	13 55	14 40	15 25
Alperton	14 15	15 00	15 45	16 30

Alan lives in Alperton. He wants to visit Parcley. He wants to spend $2\frac{1}{2}$ hours there.
- **a** What is the earliest time he could get back to Alperton?
- **b** What is the latest time he could leave Alperton?

Exercise 15.3 Real-life graphs

1. Here is a graph of a car journey.
   a. Find the distance travelled by the car after 30 minutes.
   b. Find the time the car takes to travel the first 40 km.
   c. Find the time it takes to travel the last 80 km.

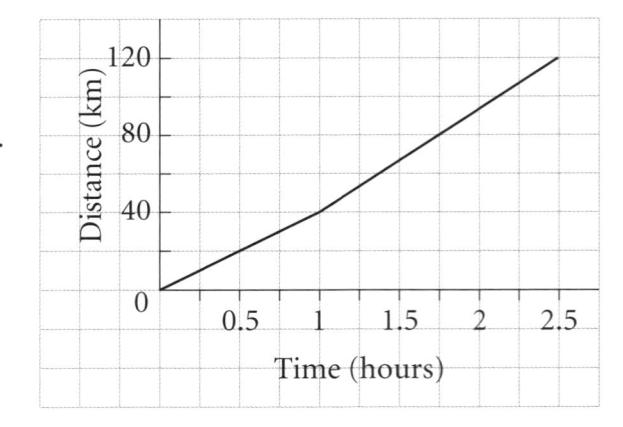

2. Melissa goes out on her bike. The graph shows her journey.
   a. How long did she take to ride the first 3 km?
   b. She stopped after 10 minutes. How can you tell this from the graph?
   c. How long did she stop for?
   d. How far had she travelled after 50 minutes?

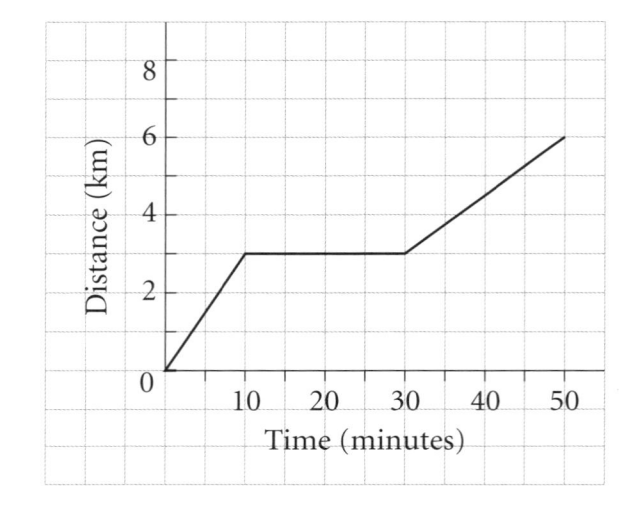

3. Jasmine went for a walk, starting from her home. This graph shows her journey.
   a. How far from home was Jasmine at 15 30?
   b. Jasmine stopped walking at 16 00. When did she start walking again?
   c. How far from home was she at 18 00?
   d. What is the total distance she walked?

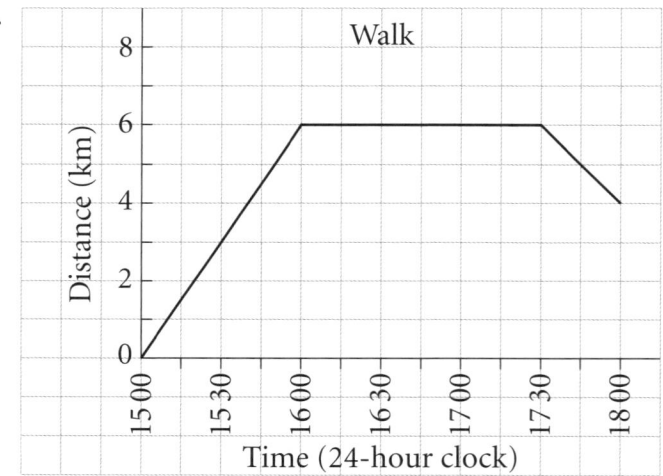

15 Time

4 Mia is filling her pool with water.
   This graph shows the depth of water in the pool.
   a Find the depth after 1 hour.
   b How long did it take to fill the first metre?
   c How long did it take to fill the last 50 cm?

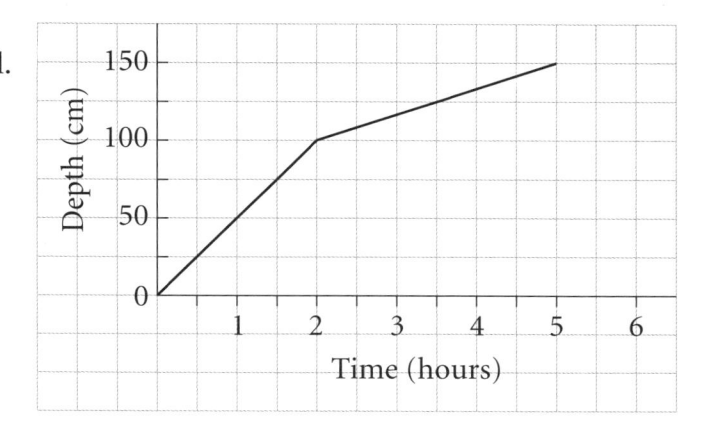

5 Simone is doing a long-distance swim.
   This graph shows the first part of her swim.
   a How far did Simone swim in the first hour?
   b In the next 2 hours she swam another 5 km.
     Copy the graph and complete it.
   c Did she swim faster in the first hour or in
     the last hour?
     Give a reason for your answer.

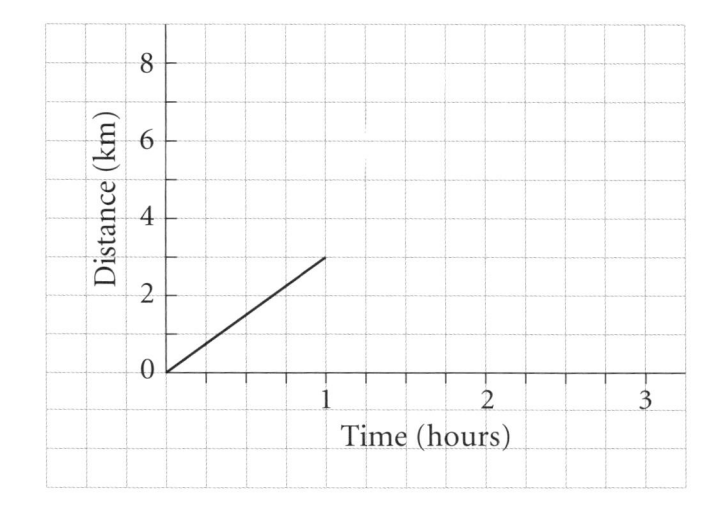

6 This graph shows the first part of Luke's
   car journey.
   a How far did the car travel in the first hour?
   b Luke stopped for one hour and then drove
     back to the start.
     The whole journey took 5 hours.
     Copy the graph and complete it.
   c Work out the total distance driven.

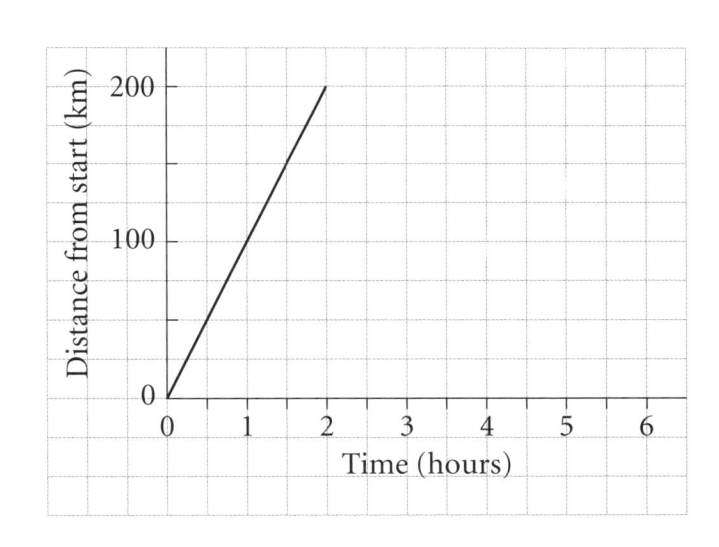

7 Hassan went for a walk.
   He walked 5 km in the first hour.
   Then he stopped for 2 hours.
   Then he walked for another hour and travelled 4 km in the same direction.
   Show Hassan's journey on a graph.

15 Time

16 Probability

◆ Exercise 16.1 The probability scale

| impossible | very unlikely | unlikely | | |
| even chance | likely | | very likely | certain |

1. Look at each outcome below.
   Choose the correct description from the box.
   a A team will win ten consecutive football matches.
   b You score at least one 6 if you throw a dice 20 times.
   c Someone runs a marathon in less than an hour.
   d You score a head when you spin a coin.
   e It will rain tomorrow if it is raining today.

2. Draw a probability scale from 0 to 1.

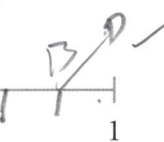

   Mark these outcomes on your scale.
   A: The probability of scoring two heads when you spin a coin twice is $\frac{1}{4}$.
   B: The probability that Seb will win a round of golf is 0.9.
   C: The probability that Morag will be late is 10%.
   D: Tomas is certain to be at the meeting.

3. Here are some possible outcomes when a dice is thrown.
   Mark them on a probability scale.
   E: The probability of throwing a 5 is $\frac{1}{6}$.
   F: The probability of throwing an odd number is $\frac{1}{2}$.
   G: The probability of scoring more than 2 is $\frac{2}{3}$.

4. The probability of sunshine tomorrow is 20%.
   The probability of rain tomorrow is double the probability of sunshine.
   The probability of cloud tomorrow is double the probability of rain.
   Mark the probabilities of sunshine, rain and cloud on a probability scale.

5.
   > The probability that my team will win tomorrow's game is 0.6.
   > The probability that my team will win at least one of the next four matches is double that.

   Xavier must be wrong.
   Explain why.

76 16 Probability

◆ Exercise 16.2 Equally likely outcomes

1 Shen chooses a letter at random from the word PROBABILITY.
Write down the probability that the letter is:
  a Y   **b** B   **c** a vowel
  d M   **e** in the word PROBABLY.

> The vowels are A, E, I, O, U.

2 In the game of Scrabble®, there are 100 tiles.
Each tile has a letter on it.
9 tiles have the letter A, 12 have E and 8 have O.
There is just one Z.
Lynn takes out one tile without looking.
What is the probability that it is:
  a a Z   **b** an A   **c** an E or an O?

3 There are 20 cards in a pack.
They are numbered from 1 to 20.
One card is taken at random. Find the probability that it is:
  a 5   **b** less than 5   **c** a multiple of 5
  d more than 5   **e** 5^2.

> Write your answers as decimals.

4 There are 7 girls, 5 boys, 9 men and 4 women in a Tai Kwon Do class.
One person is chosen at random.
What is the probability that the person chosen is:
  a a woman   **b** male   **c** not a boy?

5 What is wrong with Sasha's argument?

> The bus will be early, on time or late. These are the only three outcomes, so the probability that the bus will be late is $\frac{1}{3}$.

6 This table shows how a group of people travel to work each day.
One person is chosen at random.
What is the probability that the person chosen:
  a travels by car   **b** does not travel by bus?

Car	Bus	Walk	Total
13	7	5	25

7 There are 12 black pens, 15 blue pens and 8 red pens in a box.
Razi takes one pen at random. What is the probability that it is:
  a black   **b** black or red   **c** not red?

8 This table shows the ages of the men and women in a fitness club.
  a A man is chosen at random. What is the probability that he is under 30?
  b A person under 30 is chosen at random. What is the probability that it is a woman?
  c One person is chosen at random from the whole group. What is the probability that it is a women who is 30 or over?

	Under 30	30 or over
Men	21	29
Women	42	8

16 Probability

Exercise 16.3 Mutually exclusive outcomes

1 Here are some possible outcomes when a dice is thrown.
E: an even number
T: a multiple of 3
F: a 5
  a Find the probability of each outcome.
  b State whether these pairs of outcomes are mutually exclusive.
    i E and T   **ii** E and F   **iii** T and F

2 Chloe chooses a letter of the alphabet at random.
Here are some possible outcomes.
X: the letter is in the word ADD.
Y: the letter is in the word SUBTRACT.
Z: The letter is in the word MULTIPLY.
Say whether the outcomes in each pair are mutually exclusive. Give a reason.
  a X and Y   **b** X and Z   **c** Y and Z

3 One person is chosen from a class of students. Here are some possible outcomes.
A: The person is over 14 years old   B: The person is less than 12 years old.
C: The person is female.   D: The person is male.
For each of these statements, decide whether it is true (T), false (F) or you cannot tell (X).
  a A and B are mutually exclusive.
  b A and C are mutually exclusive.
  c C and D are mutually exclusive.

4 A dice has 12 faces, numbered from 1 to 12.
It is thrown once and the number is recorded.
Decide whether these pairs of outcomes are mutually exclusive.
If they are not, state a number that is in both outcomes.
  a The number is even.   The number is odd.
  b The number is a multiple of 4.   The number is a multiple of 5.
  c The number is a multiple of 3.   The number is a multiple of 4.
  d The number is a prime number.   The number is a square number.

5 A computer generates a random number, in the range from 1 to 100 inclusive.
  a Find the probability of each of these outcomes.
  A: it is a multiple of 9.
  B: it is a multiple of 11.
  C: It is a factor of 100.
  b State whether the outcomes in each pair are mutually exclusive.
    i A and B   **ii** A and C   **iii** B and C

16 Probability

Exercise 16.4 Estimating probabilities

1 Issa catches a minibus to work.
Each day, she records whether the minibus is early, on time or late.
Here are her results for 20 days.
Use these results to estimate the probability that tomorrow the minibus will:
  a be on time   **b** be early   **c** not be late.

Give your answers as percentages.

Early	4
On time	14
Late	2

2 A survey of the vehicles using a road during the day gave these results.

Vehicle	Car	Van	Lorry	Motorbike	Total
Frequency	83	31	18	12	144

Find the experimental probability that a vehicle is:
  a a car   **b** a motor bike   **c** a van or a lorry.

3 Vladimir uses a computer to simulate throwing three dice.
The program throws the dice 1000 times and records the number of sixes thrown each time.
Here are the results.

Number of sixes	0	1	2	3	Total
Frequency	570	350	76	4	1000

From Vladimir's results, find the experimental probability that, when you throw three dice, you will get:
  a no sixes   **b** 3 sixes   **c** 2 or 3 sixes   **d** at least 1 six.

4 Sonya spins a coin until she gets a head.
She records the number of spins required.
She repeats this 100 times.
Here is a summary of her results.

Number of throws to get a head	1	2	3	4	5	6	More than 6
Frequency	47	26	15	5	4	1	2

Estimate the probability that the number of spins needed to get a head is:
  a 1   **b** 3 or less   **c** 3 or more.

5 Samira checks the weather every Monday morning.
He records it as sunny, cloudy or wet.
Here are the results for the last 20 Mondays.

Sunny	5
Cloudy	12
Wet	3

  a Use the data to estimate the probability that
  the following Monday will be:
   i sunny   **ii** wet   **iii** cloudy or wet.
  b Why might this not be a reliable way to estimate those probabilities?

6 Susilo is using a computer program that simulates throwing a dice.
After 500 throws he has these results.

Score on the dice	1	2 or 3	4, 5 or 6
Frequency	90	155	255

  a Find the experimental probability for each of the three possible outcomes.
  b Find the theoretical probability for each of the three outcomes.
  c Do you think the computer program is reliable? Give a reason for your answer.

7 Out of 35 road accidents in a particular area in one year, eight caused serious injuries.
  a Estimate the probability that an accident will result in a serious injury.
  b The following year there were 27 accidents and 10 caused serious injuries.
  Use these figures to produce a revised estimate of the probability that an accident will result in a serious injury.

17 Position and movement

Exercise 17.1 Reflecting shapes

1 Which diagrams show a correct reflection of triangle A?

   a   b

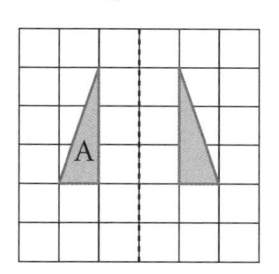

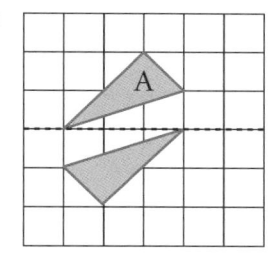

   c 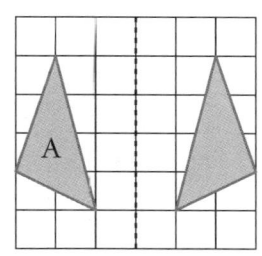   d

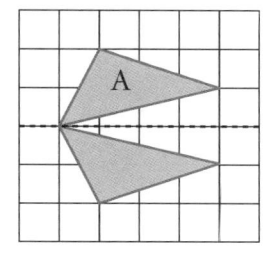

2 Copy each diagram and reflect the shape in the mirror line.

   a   b

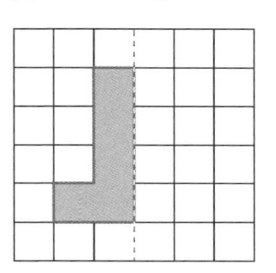

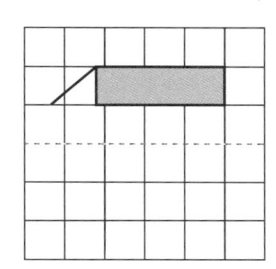

   c 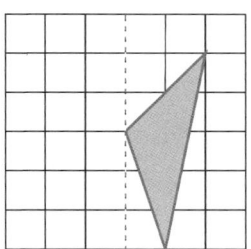   d

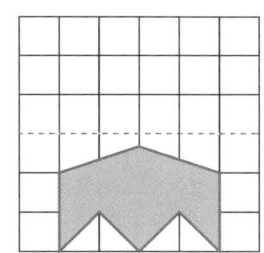

3 Copy each diagram and reflect the shape in the diagonal mirror line.

   a   b 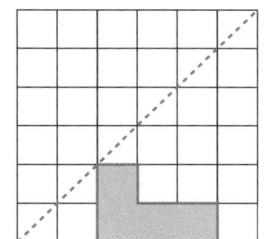   c 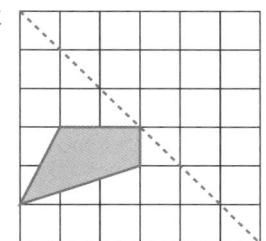   d

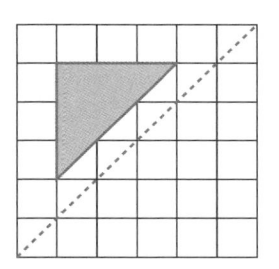

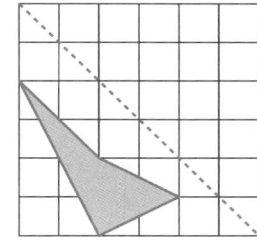

4 Copy each diagram and reflect the shape in the mirror line with the given equation.

a Mirror line $x = 3$

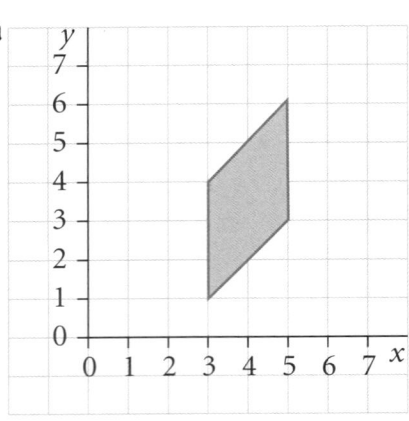

b Mirror line $y = 4$

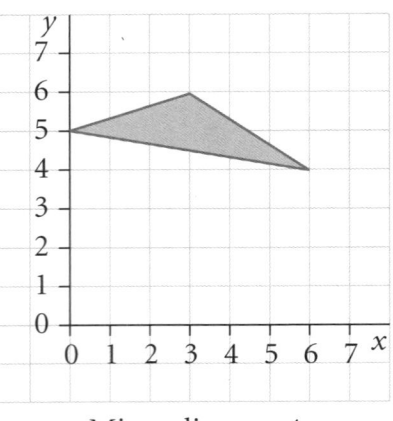

c Mirror line $x = 4$

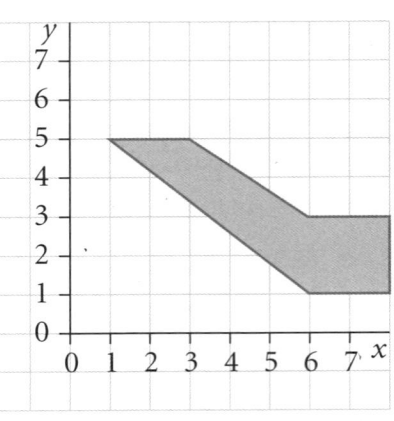

5 Copy each diagram and draw in the correct mirror line for each reflection.

a **b** 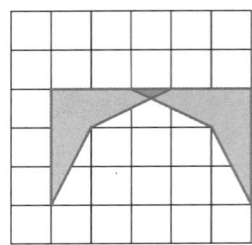 **c** 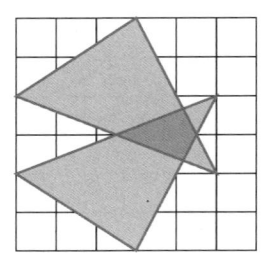 **d**

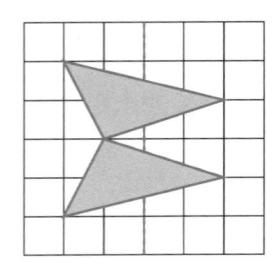

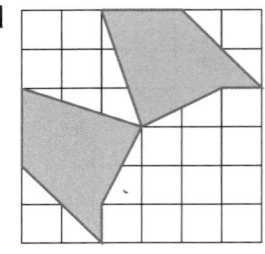

6

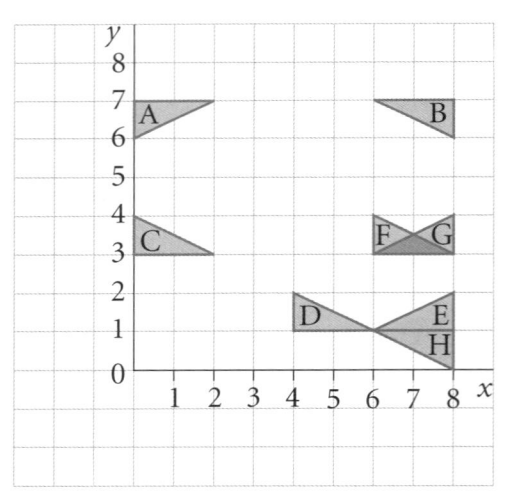

The diagram shows eight triangles A to H.
Write down the <u>equation</u> of the mirror line that reflects:
- **a** triangle A to triangle B
- **b** triangle C to triangle A
- **c** triangle E to triangle B
- **d** triangle D to triangle E
- **e** triangle G to triangle H
- **f** triangle F to triangle G.

82   **17** Position and movement

◆ **Exercise 17.2** **Rotating shapes**

1 Copy each diagram and rotate the shape about the centre C by the given number of degrees.

a 180°
b 90° anticlockwise
c 90° clockwise
d 180°

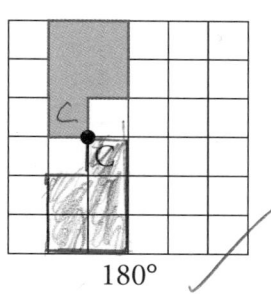

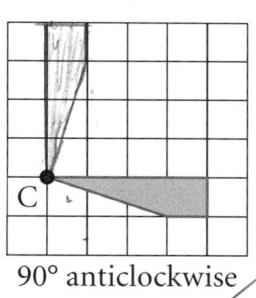

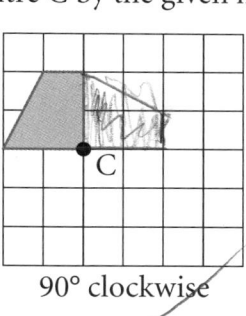

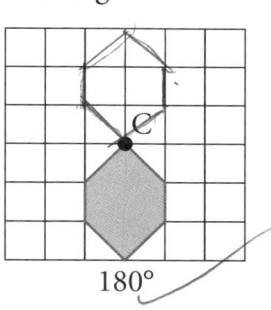

2 Copy each diagram and rotate the shape about the centre C by the given fraction of a turn.

a $\frac{1}{2}$ turn
b $\frac{1}{4}$ turn clockwise
c $\frac{1}{2}$ turn
d $\frac{1}{4}$ turn anticlockwise

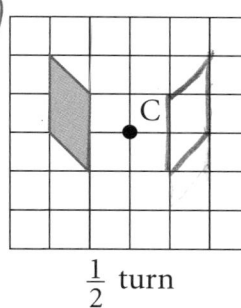

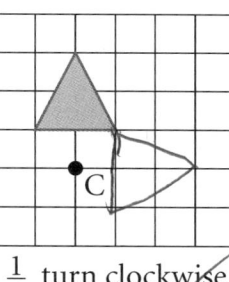

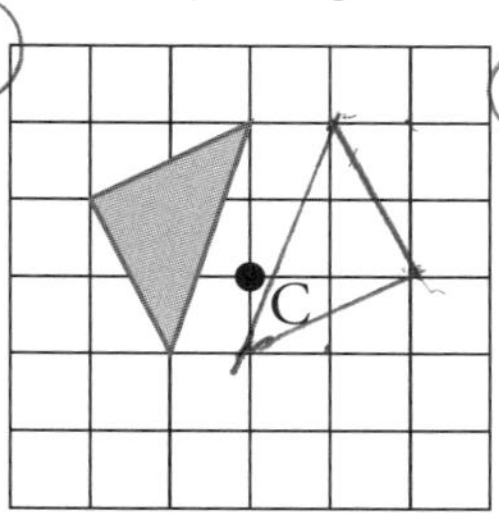

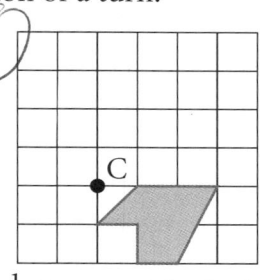

3 Copy each diagram and rotate the shape, using the given information.

a 90° anticlockwise centre (2, 4)
b 180° centre (2, 3)
c 90° clockwise centre (2, 2)
d 180° centre (3, 3)

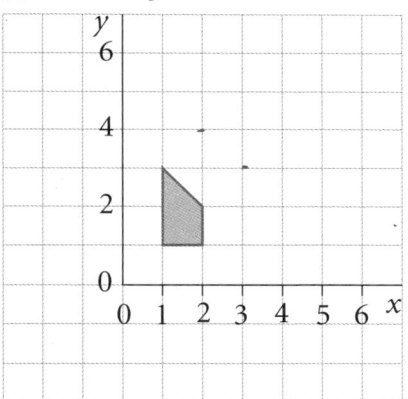

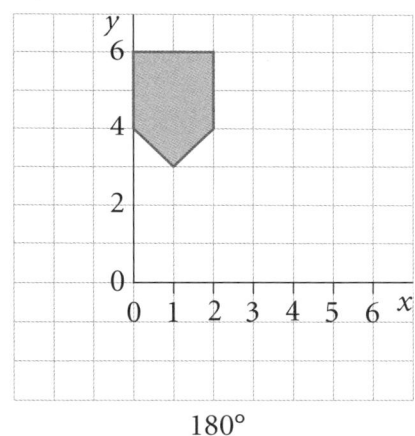

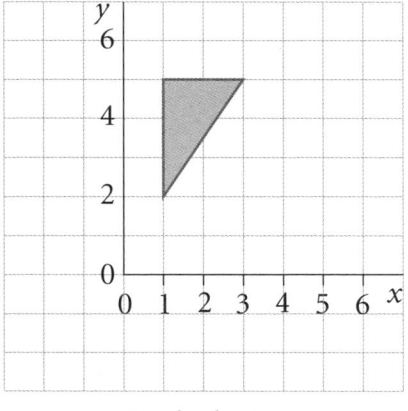

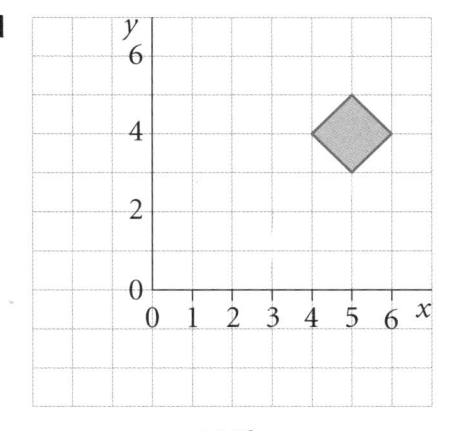

17 Position and movement　83

4 The diagram shows seven triangles.

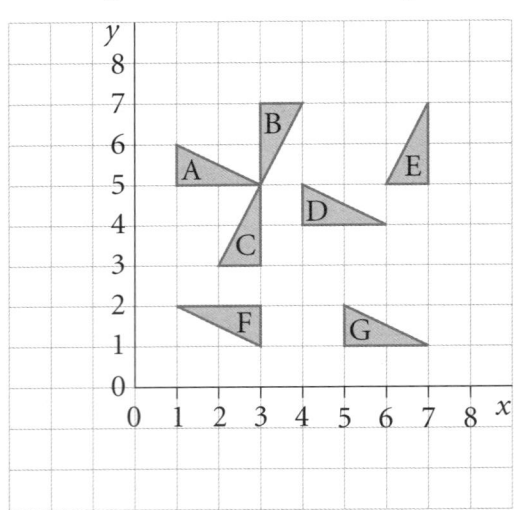

To describe a rotation you need to state:
1 the number of degrees or fraction of a turn
2 whether the turn is clockwise or anticlockwise, unless the turn is 180°
3 the coordinates of the centre of rotation.

Describe the rotation that takes:
a triangle A to triangle B
b triangle B to triangle C
c triangle C to triangle D
d triangle D to triangle F
e triangle B to triangle E
f triangle F to triangle G.

5 a Copy this diagram.
Follow these instructions to make a pattern.

1 Rotate the pattern $\frac{1}{4}$ turn anticlockwise about the centre C.
2 Draw the image.
3 Rotate the image $\frac{1}{4}$ turn anticlockwise about the centre C.
4 Draw the image.
5 Rotate the image $\frac{1}{4}$ turn anticlockwise about the centre C.
6 Draw the image.

b What is the order of rotational symmetry of the completed pattern?

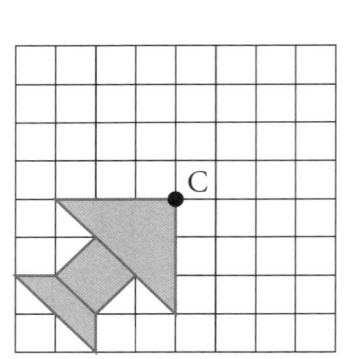

Exercise 17.3 Translating shapes

1 Copy each diagram then draw the image of the object, using the translation given.

a

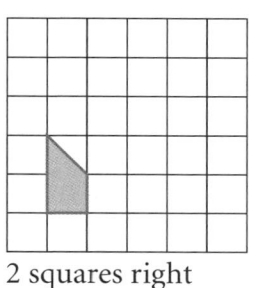

2 squares right
2 squares up

b

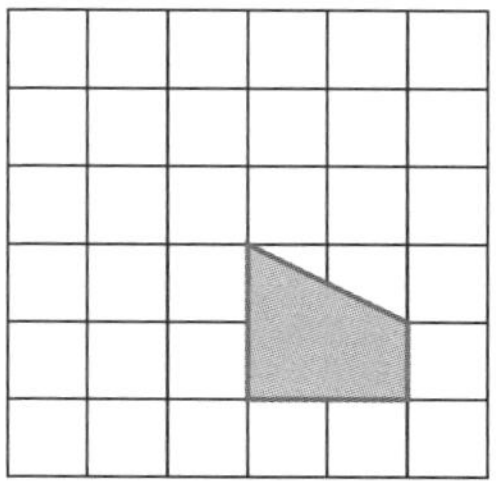

3 squares left
3 squares up

c

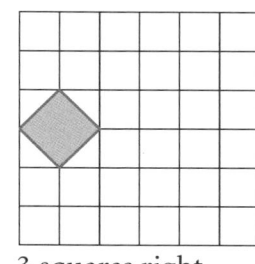

3 squares right
1 square up

d

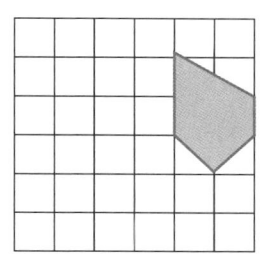

4 squares left
2 squares down

2 The diagram shows three triangles.
   Describe the translation that takes:
   a triangle A to triangle B
   b triangle B to triangle C
   c triangle C to triangle A.

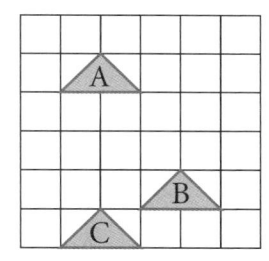

3 Copy the diagram.
   a Translate shape A 3 squares right and 2 squares up.
     Label the image B.
   b Translate shape B 2 squares right and 1 squares up.
     Label the image C.
   c Describe the translation that takes shape A to shape C.
   d Explain how you could work out the answer to part c
     without drawing shape B.

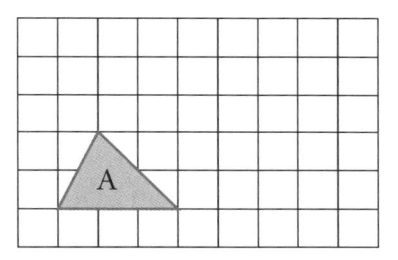

4 Alicia is giving Hassan some instructions for a translation.

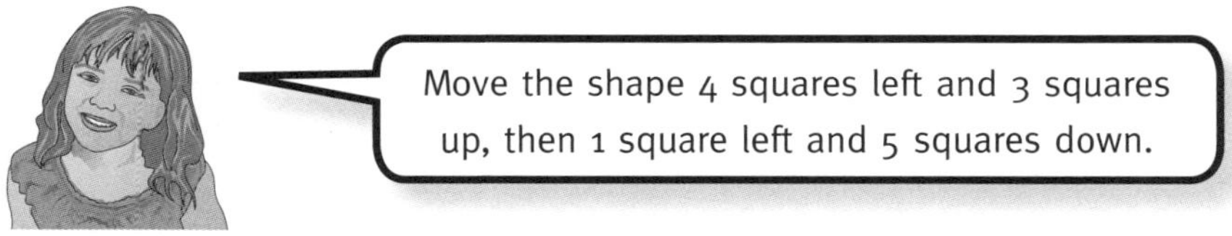

Move the shape 4 squares left and 3 squares up, then 1 square left and 5 squares down.

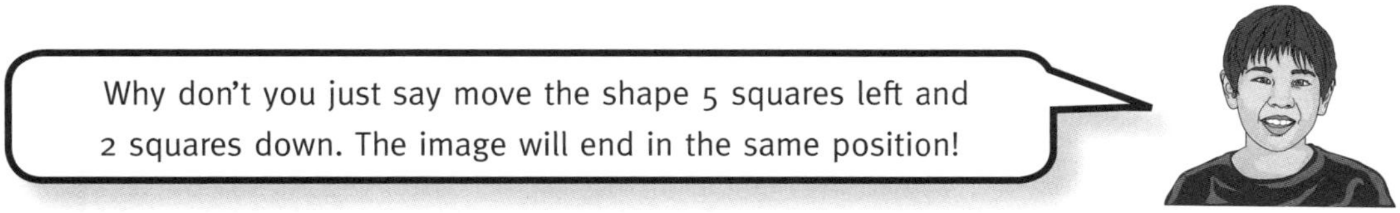

Why don't you just say move the shape 5 squares left and 2 squares down. The image will end in the same position!

Is Hassan correct?
Explain your answer.

17 Position and movement

5 Copy these coordinate axes.

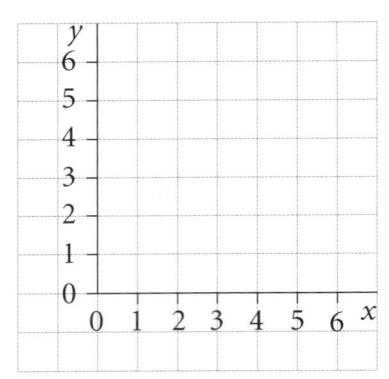

Plot and join the points A(0, 4), B(2, 3) and C(1, 6).
 a Draw the image of ABC after a translation of 4 squares right and 3 squares down.
   Label the image PQR.
 b Describe the translation that would take PQR back to ABC.
 c What do you notice about your answers to parts b and c?

6 Narek draws a triangle A onto a coordinate grid.
He draws the image of triangle A onto the grid after a translation of 3 squares left and 2 squares up.
He labels the image B.
He draws the image of triangle B onto the grid after a translation of 1 square right and 3 squares up.
He labels the image C.
 a Describe the translation that takes triangle A directly to triangle C.
 b Describe the translation that takes triangle C directly back to triangle A.

7 Dakarai shows this diagram to Harsha.

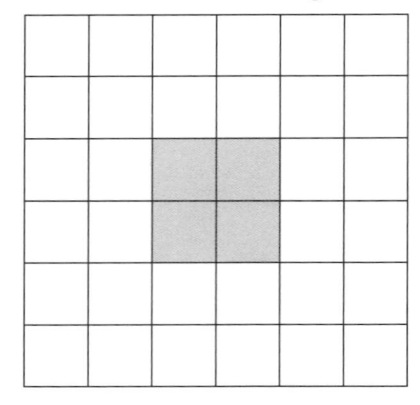

He asks Harsha to translate the shape 2 squares across and 3 squares down.
Harsha says that it's not possible as his instructions are not good enough.

Explain why Harsha is right.

17 Position and movement

18 Area, perimeter and volume

Exercise 18.1 Converting between units for area

1. What units would you use to measure the area of:
   a a thumb nail   **b** a calculator   **c** an island   **d** a rugby pitch?

2. Copy and complete the following area conversions.
   a 50 000 cm² = ☐ m²
   b 51 000 cm² = ☐ m²
   c 251 000 cm² = ☐ m²
   d 4 cm² = ☐ mm²
   e 6.8 cm² = ☐ mm²
   f 8 m² = ☐ cm²
   g 3.5 m² = ☐ cm²
   h 100 mm² = ☐ cm²
   i 455 mm² = ☐ cm²

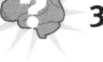

3. Yuuma says that an area of 75 000 mm² is the same as 750 m².
   Yuuma has made a mistake. Explain what mistake Yuuma has made.

Exercise 18.2 Calculating the area and perimeter of rectangles

1. Work out the area of each of these rectangles.

   a 6 m by 8 m   **b** 3 cm by 7 cm   **c** 10 mm by 22 mm

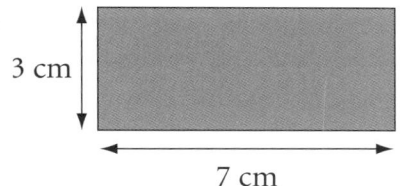

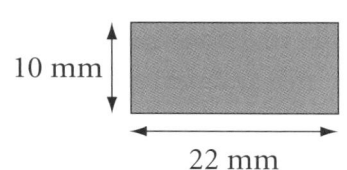

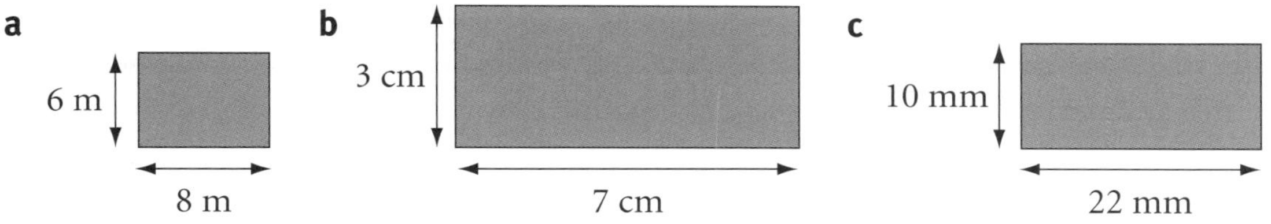

2. Work out the perimeter of each of these rectangles.

   a 5 mm by 12 mm   **b** 2 m by 3.5 m   **c** 10 cm by 40 cm

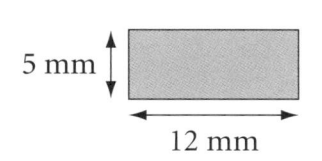

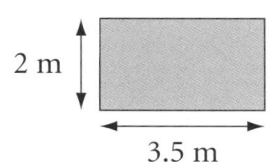

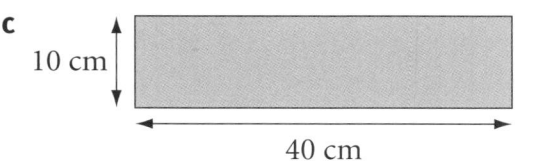

3. The screen of a laptop computer is 310 mm long and 226 mm wide.
   What is the area of the laptop screen?

4. A shop window is 5 m long and has an area of 15 m².
   a What is the height of the window?
   b What is the perimeter of the window?

5. This rectangle has a width of 7 mm and a length of 3 cm.
   a Work out the area of the rectangle. Give your answer in mm².
   b Work out the area of the rectangle again. Give your answer in cm².

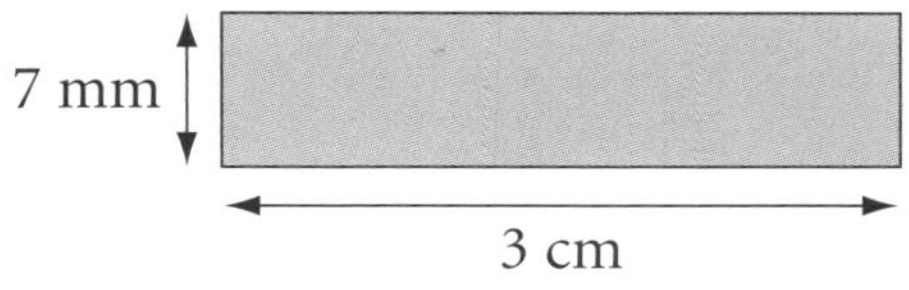

6 The table shows some information about five rectangles A to E.
   Copy and complete the table.

Rectangle	Length	Width	Area	Perimeter
A	3 cm	15 cm		
B		3 m	21 m²	
C	8 mm		40 mm²	
D	5 mm			24 mm
E		2.5 m		15 m

7 Aruzhan wants to buy a new rug for her hall.
   The rug must be 3 metres long by 70 cm wide.
   Work out the area of rug that she needs.

8 Mia and Razi are drawing rectangles with whole-number lengths and widths.

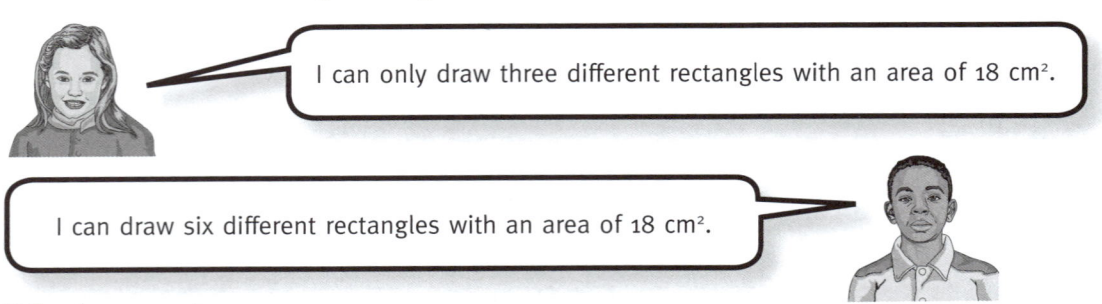

   I can only draw three different rectangles with an area of 18 cm².

   I can draw six different rectangles with an area of 18 cm².

   Who is correct?
   Explain your answer.

Exercise 18.3 Calculating the area and perimeter of compound shapes

1 Work out the area and perimeter of each of these compound shapes.

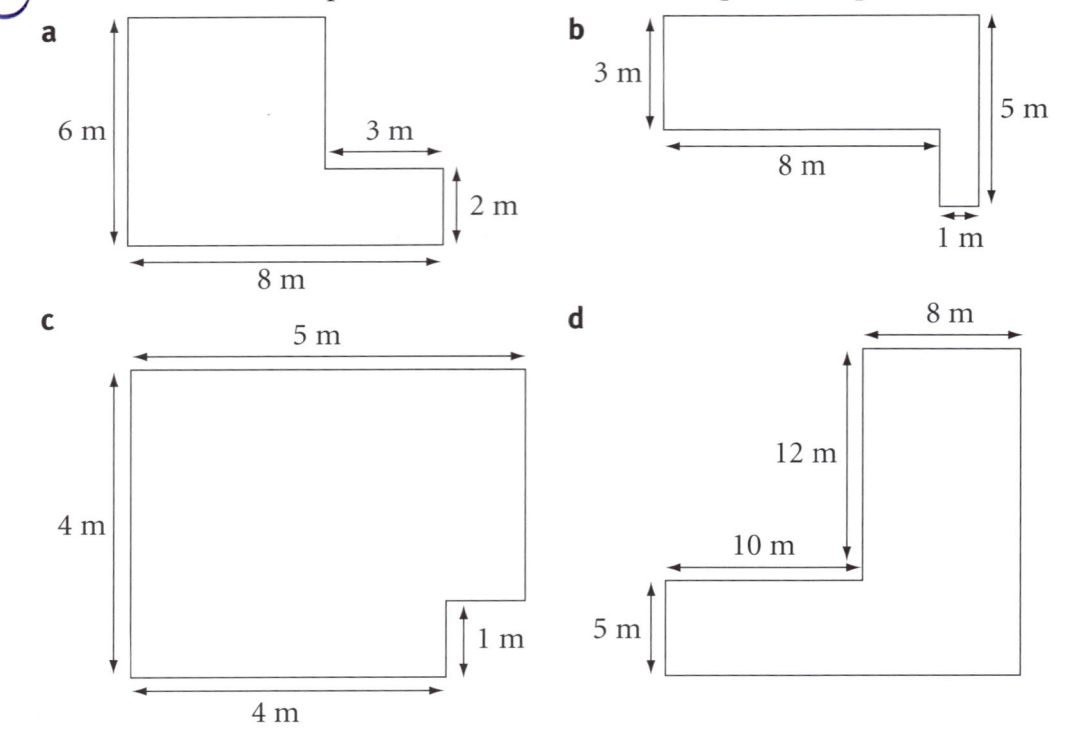

a 6 m, 3 m, 2 m, 8 m

b 3 m, 5 m, 8 m, 1 m

c 5 m, 4 m, 1 m, 4 m

d 8 m, 12 m, 10 m, 5 m

88   18 Area, perimeter and volume

2 Work out the shaded area in each of these diagrams.

a

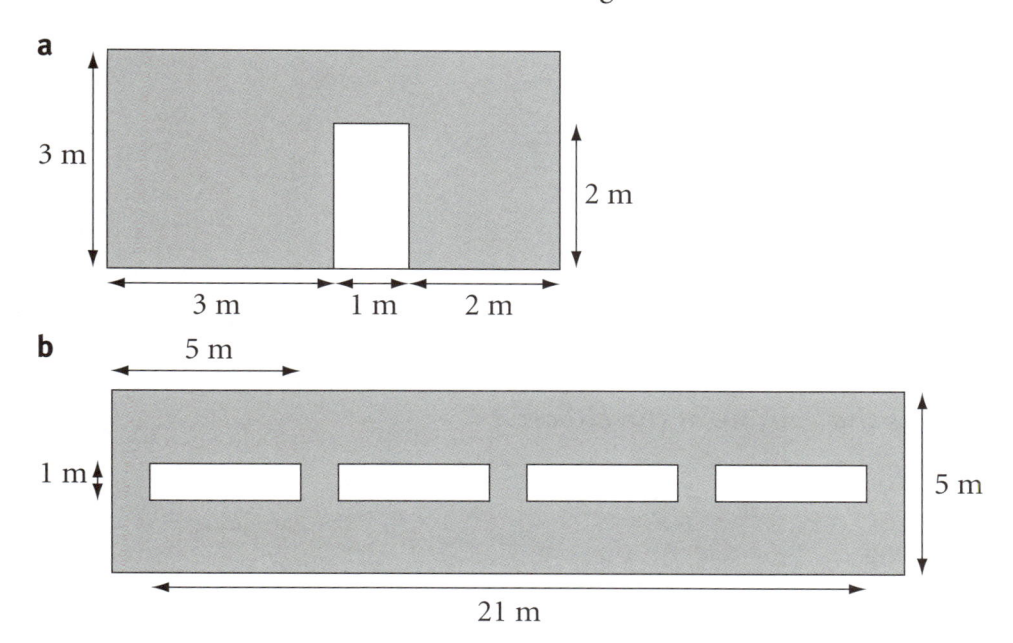

b

3 This is part of Jake's homework.

Question Work out the area and perimeter of this compound shape.

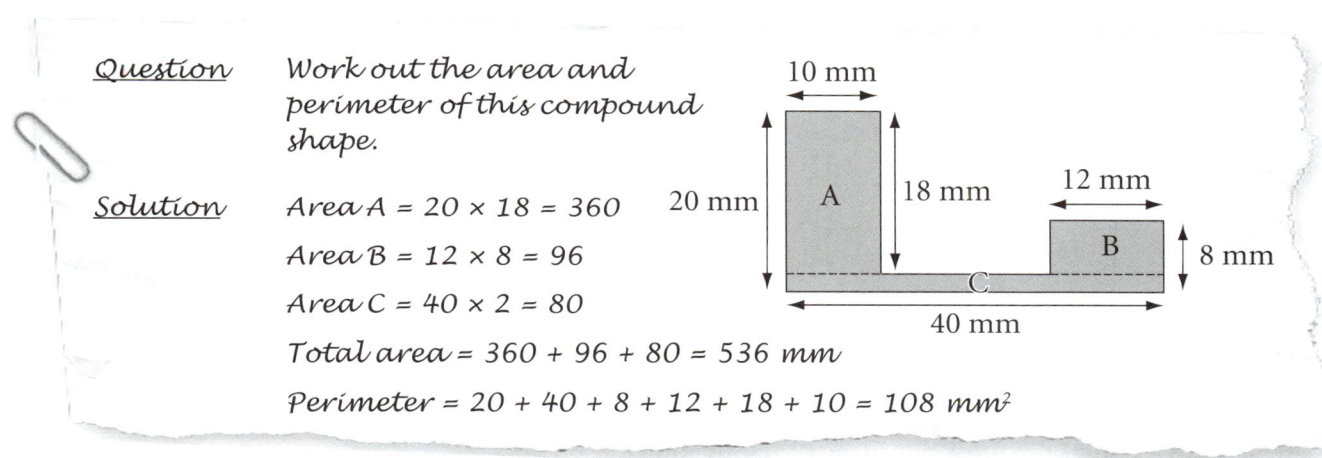

Solution Area A = 20 × 18 = 360
Area B = 12 × 8 = 96
Area C = 40 × 2 = 80
Total area = 360 + 96 + 80 = 536 mm
Perimeter = 20 + 40 + 8 + 12 + 18 + 10 = 108 mm²

Jake has made several mistakes.
Explain what he has done wrong.
Work out the correct answers for him.

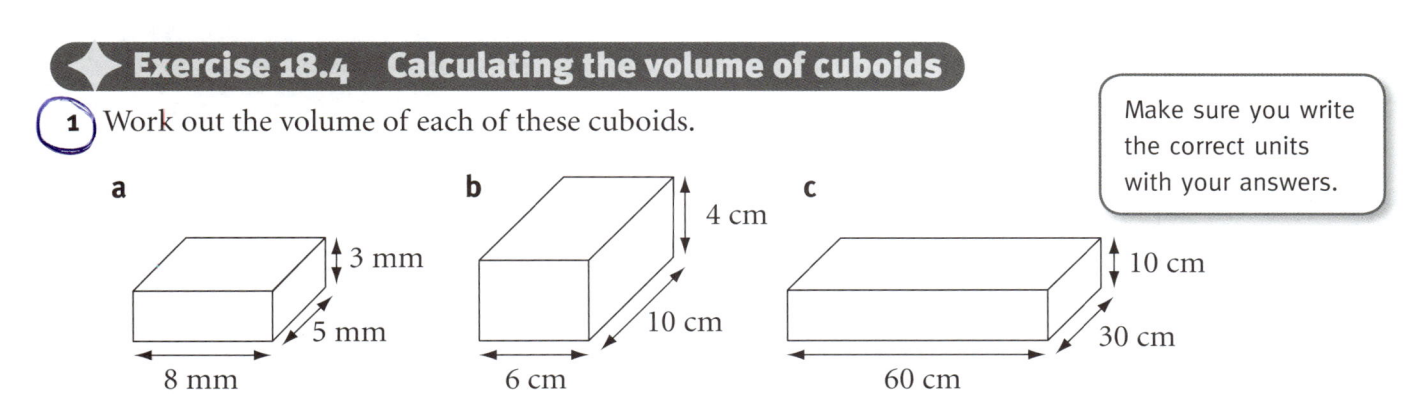

Exercise 18.4 Calculating the volume of cuboids

1 Work out the volume of each of these cuboids.

Make sure you write the correct units with your answers.

a

b

c

18 Area, perimeter and volume

2   Work out the volume of each of these cuboids.

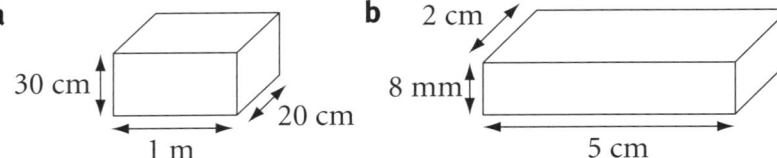

   a 30 cm, 1 m, 20 cm

   b 2 cm, 8 mm, 5 cm

3   Mrs Beecham is marking Razi's homework.

   Question A cuboid has a length of 1 m, a width of 10 cm and a height of 2 cm. What is the volume of the cuboid?

   Solution Volume = 1 × 10 × 2 = 20 m³.

   Razi has got the solution wrong.
   Explain the mistake that Razi has made
   and work out the correct answer for him.

4   The table shows the lengths, widths and heights of four cuboids.
   Copy and complete the table.

	Length	Width	Height	Volume
a	5 cm	50 mm	5 mm	☐ mm³
b	8 cm	4 cm	5 mm	☐ cm³
c	50 cm	60 cm	4 m	☐ m³
d	2.2 m	15 cm	30 cm	☐ cm³

5   A marble cuboid has a length of 1.9 m, a width of 0.8 m and a height of 5.8 m.
   a Work out the volume of the cuboid.   b Use estimation to check your answer.

6   Nadia buys a fish tank. The dimensions of the fish tank are shown in the diagram.
   Nadia fills the tank with water to $\frac{3}{4}$ of the height of the tank.
   She knows that 1 cm³ of water has a mass of 1 gram.
   What is the mass of the water in the fish tank?
   Give your answer in kilograms.

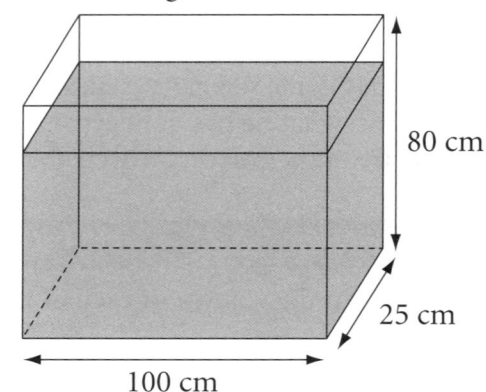

   80 cm, 25 cm, 100 cm

18 Area, perimeter and volume

Exercise 18.5 Calculating the surface area of cubes and cuboids

1 Work out the surface area of these cuboids.

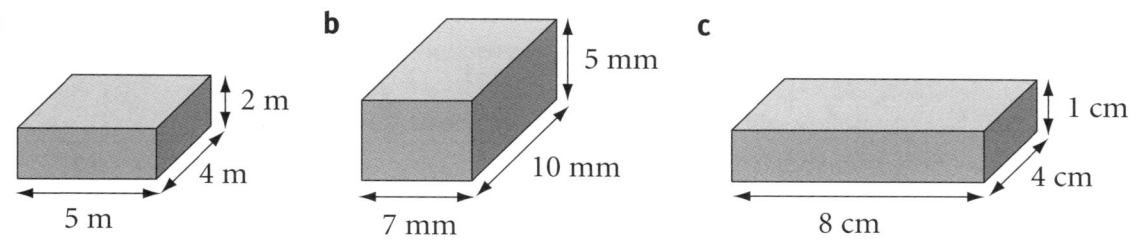

a: 5 m × 4 m × 2 m

b: 7 mm × 10 mm × 5 mm

c: 8 cm × 4 cm × 1 cm

2 Which of these shapes has the smaller surface area, the cube **A** or the cuboid **B**? Show your working.

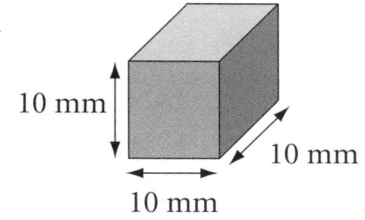

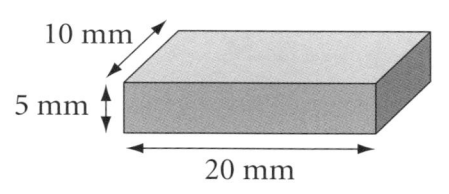

A: 10 mm × 10 mm × 10 mm

B: 20 mm × 10 mm × 5 mm

3 Which of these shapes has the smaller surface area, the cube **A** or the cuboid **B**? Show your working.

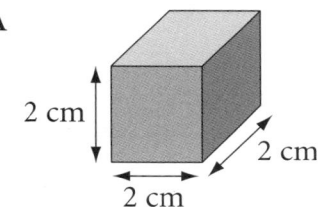

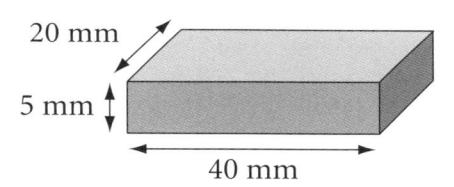

A: 2 cm × 2 cm × 2 cm

B: 40 mm × 20 mm × 5 mm

4 a Work out the surface area of this cuboid.

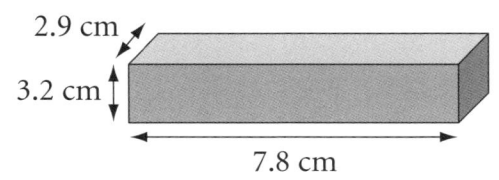

7.8 cm × 3.2 cm × 2.9 cm

b Show how to use estimation to check your answer to part **a**.

5 Work out the surface area of this cuboid.
Give your answer in:
a square cm
b square m.

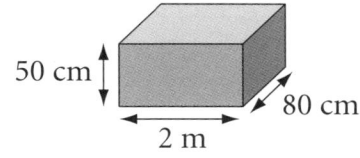

2 m × 80 cm × 50 cm

6 Emma has a wooden sculpture in the shape of a cuboid. The sculpture is 2.2 m high, 1.1 m wide and 0.55 m thick. Emma plans to paint all the faces of the sculpture with three coats of wood varnish.
a How many tins of wood varnish does Emma need to buy?
b What is the total cost of the wood varnish?

varnish $ 3.99

(Size of tin: 100 ml)
20 m² per litre

18 Area, perimeter and volume   **91**

19 Interpreting and discussing results

Exercise 19.1 Interpreting and drawing pictograms, bar charts, bar-line graphs and frequency diagrams

1. The pictogram shows how many CDs were sold in a shop in one week.
   a. How many CDs were sold on Monday?
   b. How many CDs were sold on Tuesday?
   c. How many more CDs were sold on Saturday than on Friday?
   d. How many CDs were sold in the whole week?

Day	CDs sold
Monday	◉ ◉
Tuesday	◉ ◖
Wednesday	◉
Thursday	◉ ◉
Friday	◉ ◉ ◉
Saturday	◉ ◉ ◉ ◉ ◉ ◉ ◖

   Key: ◉ represents 10 CDs

2. The table on the right shows the number of texts Maria received each day from Monday to Friday.

Day of week	Number of texts
Monday	9
Tuesday	10
Wednesday	5
Thursday	10
Friday	11

   a. Copy and complete the pictogram to show the information.
      Use the key given.

Day	Text received
Monday	⬠ ⬠
Tuesday	
Wednesday	
Thursday	
Friday	

   Key: ⬠ represents 5 texts

   b. Copy and complete the bar chart to show the information.

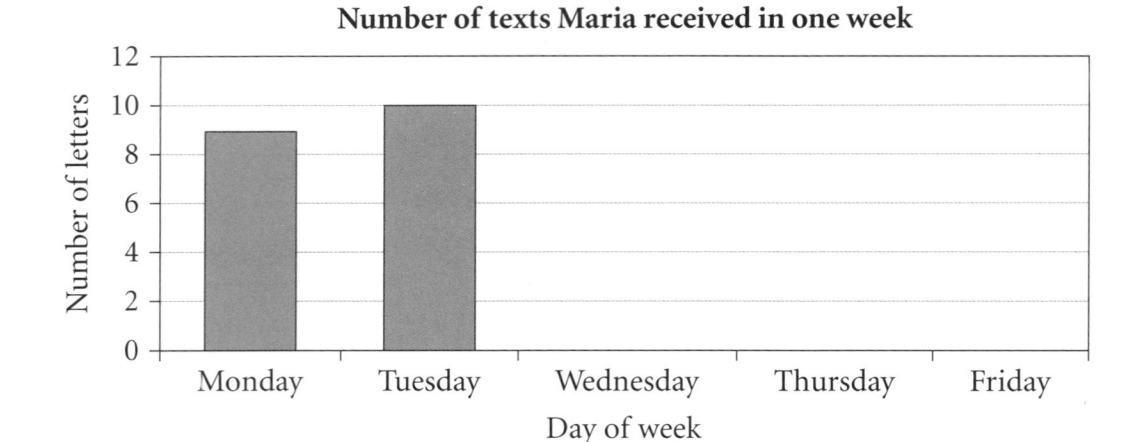

   Number of texts Maria received in one week

3 The bar-line graph shows the types of paintings sold in a gallery in one month.

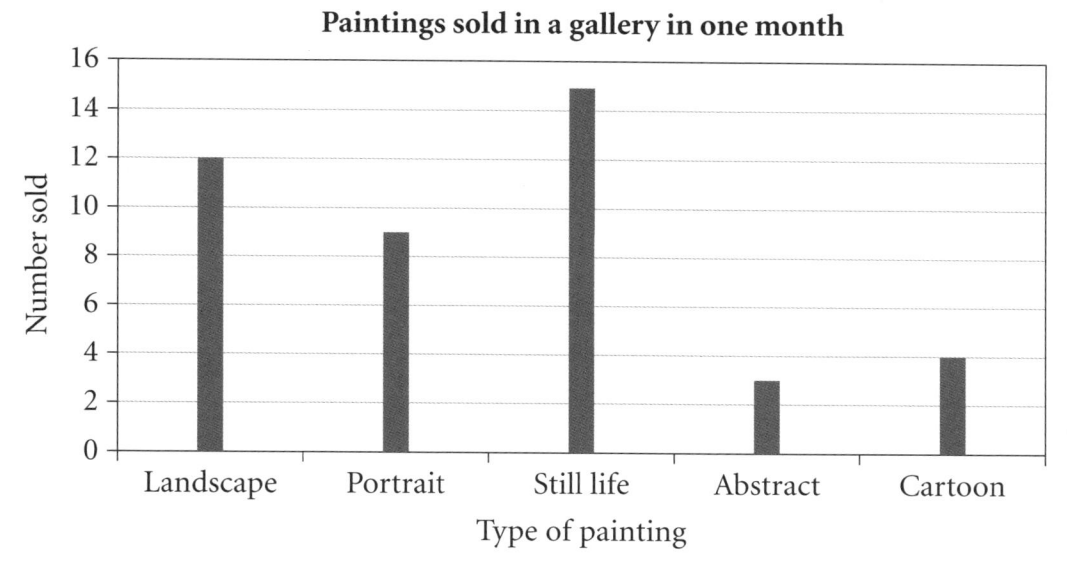

Paintings sold in a gallery in one month

a How many portrait paintings were sold?
b More still-life than abstract paintings paintings were sold.
  How many more was this?
c How many paintings were sold altogether?

4 A museum has a collection of small ammonites.
The curator measured the diameter of each one, to the nearest mm.
He recorded the results in a table, like this.
Copy and complete the frequency diagram to show the information.

Diameter of ammonite (mm)	Frequency
1–20	3
21–40	15
41–60	9
61–80	4

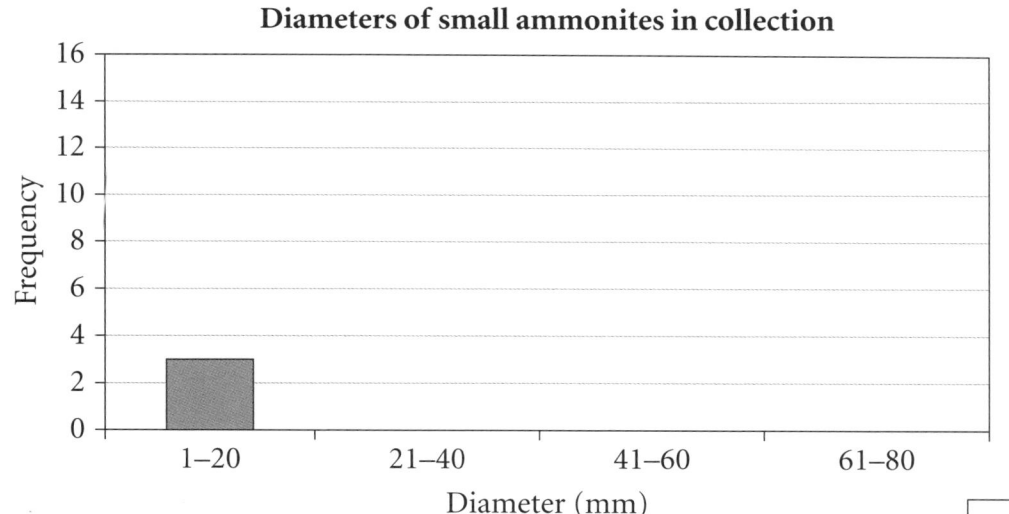

Diameters of small ammonites in collection

5 The pictogram shows the colours of the pens in a teacher's drawer.
The teacher has 16 red pens in the drawer.
How many pens are there in the teacher's drawer?
Show your working.

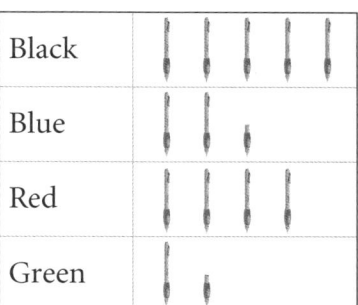

19 Interpreting and discussing results

◆ Exercise 19.2 Interpreting and drawing pie charts

1. The pie chart shows the favourite sports of a group of 100 boys.
   a. Which sport is the most popular?
   b. Which sport is the least popular?
   c. Which sports are equally popular?
   d. Explain how you can tell from the pie chart that rugby is the favourite sport of 50 of the boys.

   Boys' favourite sports

2. The pie chart shows the favourite sports of a group of girls.
   a. Which sport is the most popular?
   b. Which sport is the least popular?
   c. Which sports are equally popular?
   d. Explain why you cannot tell how many girls preferred football.

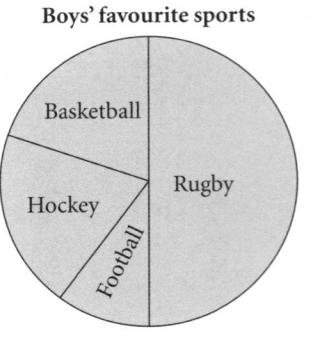

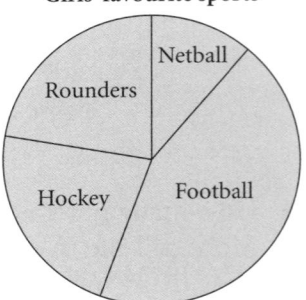

   Girls' favourite sports

3. The table shows the number of different brands of TVs in a shop.
   a. Copy and complete the calculations below to work out the number of degrees for each sector of a pie chart.

Brand of TV	Frequency
Panasonic	18
Samsung	12
Logik	2
Philips	8

   Total number of TVs = 18 + 12 + 2 + 8 = ☐ TVs
   Number of degrees per TV = 360 ÷ ☐ = ☐°
   Number of degrees for each sector:
   Panasonic = 18 × ☐° = ☐°   Samsung = 12 × ☐° = ☐°
   Logik = 2 × ☐° = ☐°   Phillips = 8 × ☐° = ☐°

   b. Draw a pie chart to show the information in the table.

4. A group of 90 people were asked about the type of snack they preferred.
   The table shows the results.
   Draw a pie chart to show the information in the table.

Type of snack	Frequency
Crisps	35
Nuts	20
Chocolate	27
Other	8

5. Copy the table showing some students' favourite days of the week.
   a. Complete the table by working out the number of degrees for each sector of a pie chart.
   b. Draw a pie chart to show the information in the table.

Favourite day	Frequency	Number of degrees (°)
Friday	15	90
Saturday	32	
Sunday	9	
Other	4	

19 Interpreting and discussing results

◆ Exercise 19.3 Drawing conclusions

1 Jazmin and Sarah live in different streets.
The pictograms show how the adults in Jazmin's street and in Sarah's street travel to work.

Jazmin's Street	
Car	▦ ▦
Walk	▦ ▦ ▦ ▦ ▱
Bus	▱
Train	

Key: ▦ represents 4 adults

Sarah's Street	
Car	▦ ▦ ▦ ▦ ▦ ▦
Walk	▱
Bus	▦
Train	▦ ▦ ▦ ▱

Key: ▦ represents 4 adults

a Work out the number of adults in:
  i Jazmin's street **ii** Sarah's street.
b Compare the pictograms and make **two** comments.
c Do you think that the adults in Jazmin's street live near to where they work?
Explain your answer.
d Do you think that the adults in Sarah's street live near to where they work?
Explain your answer.

2 Luka carries out a survey on the favourite canteen food of some of the students in his year group at school. The bar charts show his results.

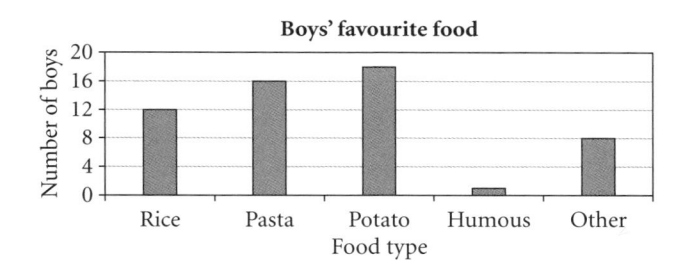

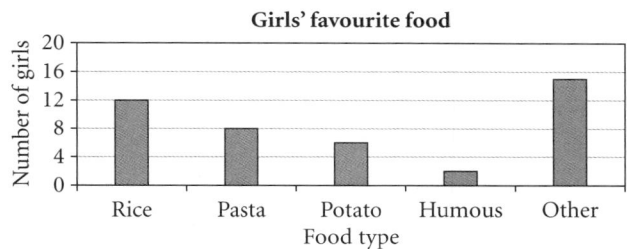

a Work out:
  i the number of boys surveyed   **ii** the number of girls surveyed.
b Give a possible reason why your two answers in part **a** are different.
c Compare the bar charts and make two comments.
d Which food type is the favourite for the same number of boys as girls?
e Which food type is the favourite of twice as many girls as boys?
f Which food type is the favourite of three times as many boys as girls?
g Write down the modal food type for:
  i the boys **ii** the girls.

> Do not include the group 'other' for part **g** of this question.

3 Mr Ree gave the students in his class a geography test and a history test.
The frequency diagrams show the results of the tests.

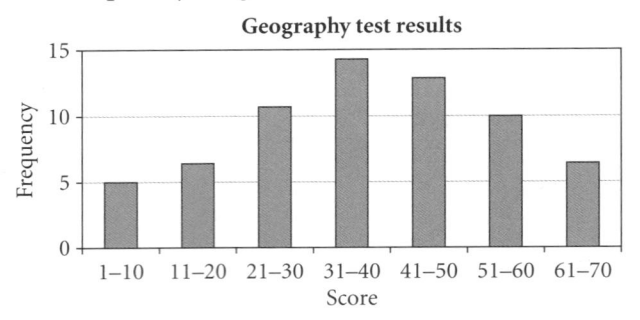

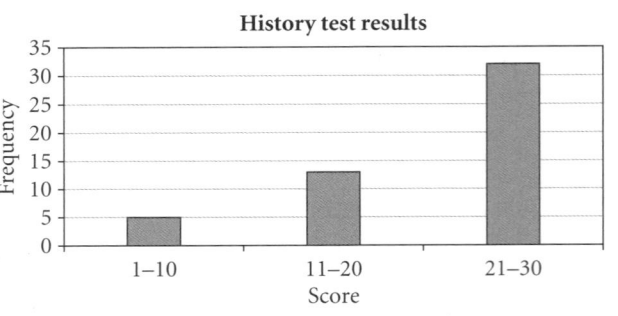

Mr Ree shows the class the frequency diagrams and asks for any questions or comments.
a Ahmad said: 'History was a harder test as the highest score was only 30 marks.'
   Why might Ahmad be wrong?
b Compare the frequency diagrams and make two comments.
c Write down the modal score for:
   i the geography test   ii the history test.

4 The pie charts show how Shen and Oditi spend their free time each weekend.

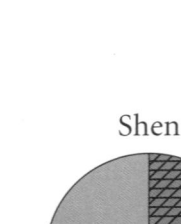

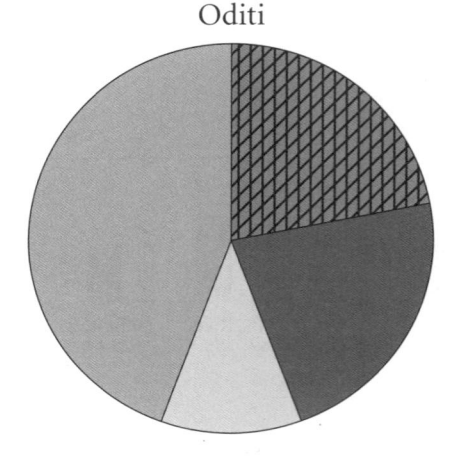

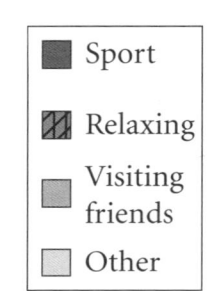

a
I spend about half as much time relaxing as Oditi does, as the 'relaxing' sector of my pie chart is about half the size of Oditi's.

Is Shen correct? Explain your answer.

b
We both spend the same proportion of our free time on sport, as our 'sports' sectors have the same angle.

Is Oditi correct? Explain your answer.

19 Interpreting and discussing results